MUSICAL INSTRUMENTS IN COLOR

Musical Instruments in Color

PETER GAMMOND

Photography Richard Bird

Macmillan Publishing Co., Inc.
New York

Macmillan Publishing Co., Inc.
866 Third Avenue, New York, N.Y. 10022

Library of Congress Cataloging in Publication Data

Gammond, Peter.
  Musical instruments in color.
  (Macmillan color series)
  1. Musical instruments. I. Title.
ML460.G22   1976   781.9'1   75-17604
ISBN 0-02-542410-0

First American Edition 1976

Color printed by Colour Reproductions, Billericay
Text printed and books bound in Great Britain by
Tinling (1973) Ltd., Prescot, Merseyside

Contents

Acknowledgments

The author and publisher wish to thank the following for their kind permission to reproduce the illustrations in this book: Boosey & Hawkes Museum, 1, 7, 10, 12, 14, 15, 16, 17, 18, 19, 21, 25, 26, 27, 28, 29, 30, 31, 32, 47, 50, 51, 58, 59, 60, 61, 62, 63, 64; Salvi, 2, 3; W. E. Hill, 4, 5, 8, 9, 11, 13, 44 (bottom), 45, 46, 48, 49 (bottom); Scarf's, 23; Horch and Co., 24; John Leach, 52, 53, 54, 55, 56, 57, 78; British Piano Museum, 43, 68, 69, 71; Indiacraft, 74, 75, 76, 77; Fenton House, 33, 34, 44 (top), 49 (top); Morley and Co., 35, 37, 38, 39, 40, 41; R. Mann, 79; Discourses Ltd., for various line drawings.

I Musical instruments: the beginnings

The full story of the growth and development of musical instruments among the primitive races must, of course, remain a subject for interesting but vain speculation. What we do know is that music had a well-established part in all the ancient civilisations – as we can see in surviving illustrations. The improvement of instruments was very slow at first. They remained quite primitive until well into the fifteenth century when the art of notating and writing music was perfected. This encouraged the gradual sophistication of instruments to match the demands of the composers.

Difficult as it is to align our own knowledge-crammed minds with the mind of primitive man, it is fascinating to let the imagination suggest what his first tentative steps in music-making may have been. Rhythmical noises must have distinguished themselves from the non-rhythmical almost as soon as man was able to think and communicate. The mystery of the heart-beat within his own body must have given rhythm a mystical significance, and surely we can assume that the exciting noises that he could make by beating or shaking natural objects must have been used in an imitative way and that dancing was a very early form of enjoyable exercise.

Primitive percussion must have been very much the same as we find it in the backward tribes of today: the clapping of hands, the clashing of sticks, the shaking of dried seeds, the scraping of a serrated edge, the beating of gourds and hollowed-out logs.

As man's perception grew he must have become aware, partly through birdsong and other natural sources and partly through his own experiments, that not all sounds were the same. He would begin to discern the difference in pitch obtained by hitting a short or a long piece of wood or stone, which probably led to the first kind of primitive xylophone.

He would discover then that a taut string of whatever material he used in his hunting bow produced a pleasant twang, again varying in pitch according to its length. Early instruments of the harp family are little more than bows, the sound being amplified by attaching the string to or passing it through a gourd or some other hollow body.

Presumably man first discovered wind instruments when he blew into a conch shell (pl. 1) or across the top of a hollow cane. Later, perhaps, came the discovery that a reed held between the fingers produced a peculiarly poignant sound when its edge was blown and vibrated.

But speculation must end there. This book is not intended as a history of musical instruments nor as a primer for their use. We will regard musical instruments as objects of practical beauty and, by understanding their natures and functions, hope to add to the enjoyment of the music they produce. Early instruments decided how music would develop; not until later, very much later, did music itself begin to force the instrument-makers to produce contraptions of the maximum flexibility.

Until comparatively recent times and the introduction of electric and electronic devices, musical instruments have remained (in four major groups – percussive, plucked, bowed and blown) simply ingenious developments of their primitive ancestors. The principles that operate the conch shell still operate the modern trumpet; the modern drum is not all that far removed from the first that man made from a stretched skin. It is this reliance upon organic materials and nature's sounds that has dictated the beautiful and natural shapes of instruments and allowed them to retain a mystical nature.

Although some of the companion volumes in this series have been written with the collector in mind, it would be unrealistic to suggest that the average person could become a collector of musical instruments. Their fragility and scarcity means that most early examples must be kept in museums. The price of an early violin like a Stradivarius (the 'Lady Blunt' Strad was sold at Sotheby's in 1971 for £84,000) puts it beyond the reach of the ordinary person, and even modern harps or bassoons now cost as much as a car. The 'collector' must simply collect experiences, enjoy looking at instruments in the many great collections that are available to him and take every opportunity to hear them played.

2

The harp

There is no logical way of plotting a course through the instruments, but the text of this book will follow the sequence of photographs that make up the main section of the book. The stringed instruments have established their place as the leading musical protagonists today, so we will start with the plucked instruments of the harp family.

Taking the basic principle that strings of varying length and thickness, stretched between two points at uniform tautness, will give you a range of notes of varying pitch, the harp seems the logical outcome. Or, from another point of view, an unnecessarily involved and cumbersome way of doing things. In other words, the harp uses one string for each note, whereas other stringed instruments worked on the principle of using fewer strings and varying their length, thus achieving a more compact shape.

There is no need, however, to regret the harp's mechanically unsophisticated nature, for its principles have produced some of the most beautiful instruments that man has devised, both to look at and to hear.

Before looking at the long and continuing development of the harp, mention must be made of an instrument that has become extinct, except in a few regions of East Africa – the lyre. In principle a harp, it lacks the potential flexibility that has kept the harp alive from the earliest times until today. The lyre has its strings running between a bar or yoke which joins two arms (sometimes in that delightfully arty shape that gives lyre-birds their name) to a sounding box from which the two arms extend. This can either be a box-like affair, as in the Greek *cithara*, or bowl-shaped (in early instruments it was often a tortoiseshell), as in the *lyra*. The lyre, as the many early illustrations of it show, was a small instrument to be held in the crook of one arm and plucked with the other hand, and it would have had a fairly weak voice. Its tuning system was primitive and insecure and its strings, of more or less uniform length, were not tuned in a scale but in an irregular sequence so that a few at a time could be used to produce various chords. It was not basically intended as a melodic instrument, but simply to accompany the voice.

Probably the harp started with the same simple ambition but it always had the potential of becoming a solo instrument because its strings provided some kind of ascending scale.

The harp utilises two basic principles: strings of varying length and thickness; and amplification through some kind of hollow sounding box. Any simple experiment will demonstrate that strings on their own tied between two solid points will not produce a sound which is satisfyingly loud, resonant or lasting. The harp, then, is basically a triangle with one side perpendicular, and the strings running parallel to this side between the other two arms of the triangle thus getting shorter towards its apex. The upper of these two arms provides a solid basis for the tuning pegs, the lower is a hollow sounding-box.

The earliest harp looked, in fact, rather more like a *mandolin* with the neck set at an angle to the body and the strings running between the two. Because this neck was often flexible and incapable of sustaining much tension the strings were fairly slack and the pitch of early harps would thus have been fairly low. By about 2500 BC the classical Greek harp was looking something like the modern instrument, already quite large, probably supported on the knee of a seated player with its perpendicular side against his body and his arms extended on either side of the instrument. This is the reverse of the modern position in which the longest strings are furthest away from the player and the sound-box is nearest to his body, and the whole is now usually of such a size that it rests upon the floor. The basic triangular shape, with the sound-box, or chest, leaning towards the player, is common to most European variants of the harp, although not to Asiatic or African instruments.

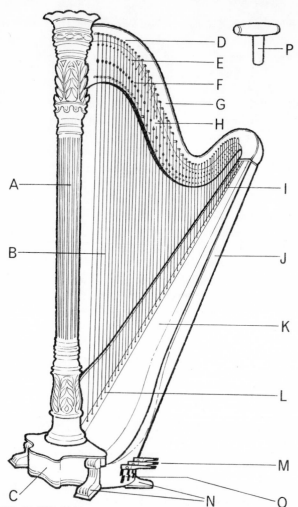

THE PARTS OF THE HARP

A Column or fore-pillar, containing the seven pedal rods. **B** Harp strings. **C** Base. **D** Tuning-pins or pegs. **E** Bridge-pins. **F** Rotating discs. **G** String arm, neck or harmonic curve. **H** Metal plate. **I** Ivory pegs. **J** Body of the harp. **K** Sound board (extended as with the concert harp). **L** Eyelets (in sound board). **M** Pedals. **N** Feet. **O** Pedal notches. **P** Tuning key.

The medieval harp, which the Irish played such a prominent part in developing, was a small instrument, ranging in height from ·6 m to 1·2 m (2 ft to 4 ft). It was essentially a portable instrument used by the travelling entertainer. It had a single row of strings tuned to the diatonic scale, and it was used to provide a simple accompaniment to traditional songs or to play uncomplicated solos.

The harmonious shape, which may look like the imaginings of a romantic painter, is purely functional. The sound-box body is basically a straight box, the side nearest to the strings being flat, the other sides rounded. Its sides are more nearly parallel in the earlier harps but get more tapered in the later instruments, with the narrowest portion at the top end where the strings are shortest. The neck, the top arm of the triangle which holds the tuning pins, has a graceful inward curve or bow. Again, this is not just artistic fancy, but is dictated by harmonic laws which are rather too complicated to go into fully but can best be explained in a negative way. If the neck were straight the strings would have to be given an uneven tension, because a graph showing the ratio of length to tension is not a straight line but a curved one; so it was discovered at a fairly early stage that the 'harmonic curve' was essential to give an even tension to the strings. Finally there is the third limb, the forepillar, which has the simple function of completing the triangle and maintaining the overall tension. In many of the earlier harps it curved gently outwards to give it strength, but in the modern harp it is generally a very sturdy straight pillar, highly decorated to disguise its robustness.

Like most early instruments, the harp had to develop or become obsolete. One rival was the *lute* (and an attractive hybrid instrument called the harp-lute), which introduced the immortal principle of varying the lengths of the strings and obtaining several notes on each, so providing an infinitely variable chromatic scale from a small instrument. Other rivals, as accompanists and soloists, were the rapidly developing keyboard instruments.

As composers demanded more notes and more complicated harmonies, the harp-makers searched for ways to make their instruments more flexible. They began by trying instruments with two or three rows of strings, one of them to provide the semitones or accidentals, but obviously this made it an incredibly difficult instrument to play. Towards the end of the seventeenth century, when harpists had already discovered that they could raise the note slightly by pressing a finger on the string close to the soundboard, a tuning device was incorporated whereby a hook on the neck could be turned to press against the string, making it tauter and raising its note by a semitone.

Such devices, however, left the harpist, like the traditional timpanist, with the problem of having to reset his instrument for each musical item demanding a key change. What was really wanted was a mechanical means of changing the pitch of the strings and restoring it while the player was still performing, and various methods were used to try and achieve this. First the primitive hooks were turned by a series of levers in the forepillar, then various other systems were tried until the modern harp was perfected, mainly in Paris and largely through the inventive genius of Sébastien Érard (1752–1831). This system, which is still in use, has brass discs with two studs which bear against the strings when turned, thus increasing their tension. The turning is done by a mechanism operated by foot-pedals at the base of the instrument, seven now being a common number, so that the player can maintain a standard fingering and use the same strings while being able to play in any key.

By this time, with the neck and the forepillar having to carry and contain so much mechanism, the harp had become a large, heavy and cumbersome instrument, far removed from the dainty object that angels are traditionally supposed to carry around. It varied between a substantial drawing-room size and the full concert 'grand' around 1·8 m (6 ft) high and often as heavy as its player.

It could be said that the harp developed just fast enough to keep itself in fashion and demand. Nineteenth-century composers and virtuosi gave it a place as a solo instrument which promoted its enormous popularity among Victorian amateurs; while composers from Berlioz onward have consistently used the harp as one of the regular instruments and colourings of modern orchestration. The harp-makers have continued to aim at perfection, and the sturdiest and most practical modern harps have come from America, notably

16

from makers in Chicago and New York.

It is fortunate that the modern development of the harp (likewise the piano) has not obliterated interest in the older and more primitive instruments; on the contrary, it has stimulated an interest in their preservation and use. The use of the Irish and Welsh harps has been continued and cultivated. One of the earliest surviving instruments is the 'Brian Boru' harp kept at Trinity College, Dublin. Although not quite as old as originally rumoured, nevertheless it probably dates back to the fourteenth century.

The drawing-room craze brought in various portable and less expensive deviants that gave an approximation of the harp's 'melting and prolonged' sounds (to quote Bacon) and tried to make life a little easier for the amateur practitioner. The *harp-lute* was a curious but delightful cross between a harp and a fretted instrument; the *harp-lyre* aimed at a full sound from moderate proportions; the *zither-harp* (still to be found in antique shops in fair numbers) provided some ready-made chords for the left hand and a set of melody strings for the right – all of them usually named on the instrument in most unprofessional fashion.

Outside Europe, the harp remained a primitive instrument, often simply a bowed shape with the strings strung across the extremities – as in a hunting bow – with one half developing into a simple sound-box. The principle of the harp, basically one string to a note plucked to produce its then amplified sound, was to be extended to a number of closely related instruments.

The fourteenth-century *psaltery* indicates one breakaway direction. Instead of the strings being extended across the harp's open frame they are extended between two rows of pegs which are inserted in what is basically a flat, resonant box. This box did not have parallel opposite sides, but became narrower at one end to accommodate the shorter strings, wider at the other end for the longer, and often with the sides showing the same 'harmonic curve' that we noted in the harp. Instruments of this kind are sometimes played upright in the arms (as the psaltery apparently was) or, more frequently, in a horizontal position on the knees or on a table with a sound hole cut in the upper surface of the box below the strings. This led to a whole range of plucked string instruments with a similar range of shape and sound, but where the strings are hit with beaters, or hammers, like the *dulcimer* and *cimbalom*. The harp is also the obvious precursor of the keyboard instruments, like the *harpsichord* and, after all, the frame of a modern grand piano is still very much like a harp laid on its side.

But, as far as the mainstream of European music is concerned, the main developments of the harp were to be those which noted its limitations and discovered more flexible ways of using plucked strings and means of sustaining a string's note by using methods of sound production other than plucking.

3

Bowed string instruments

This brings us to the most important instruments in Western music, the bowed string family. We have already noted the principle that the longer a string is the lower its note, and vice versa, and adopted the assumption that the note can be slightly varied if the tension is varied. This last attribute has only a limited application (as in the harp), because there is an ideal tension for any given string at which it gives its best and clearest sound. If it is too slack it buzzes and will probably flap against the instrument; if it is too tight it will simply break. Another principle which must be mentioned is that, again to a limited extent, the thickness of a string also dictates its pitch. Thicker strings give a lower note than thin strings at the same tension. A long thick string, at the ideal tension, will give a better low note than an even longer thin string, as well as meeting the practical consideration that its length must be limited. The fundamental laws governing these facts are that thicker and longer strings vibrate more slowly than thin short ones. The faster a string vibrates, thus setting up corresponding vibrations in the air, the higher the note that is produced.

If a small number of strings of varying thickness are stretched between two sets of pegs the same distance apart and at the ideal tension a range of notes will be obtained. If the playing length of any of these strings is shortened by pressing them at given points against the body of the instrument each will produce a progressively higher note the shorter it gets, until the thickest string produces the same note as the open string of higher pitch next to it. Then move to that string and so on up the scale, repeating the process until one reaches the highest string at its shortest length that produces a usable sound. Thus, as in the *violin*, an instrument can have a practicable range of two or three octaves from only four strings. In contrast to a harp-like instrument which would need thirty or so strings and the means of producing semitones.

This demonstrates a new principle on which stringed instruments can work. In practical terms some sort of body is needed, with pegs at either end between which to stretch a few strings of varied thickness. One end must be thin so that it can be grasped in one hand, at the same time allowing the fingers of that hand to shorten the length of the strings while the fingers of the other hand, or some implement, produce a note from the string. The lower part of the instrument needs to widen out into some kind of sound-box to amplify the feeble sound of the natural string. Thus we have the basic stringed instrument with its hollow body, complete with sound-holes, to which the vibrations of the strings are transmitted by passing over a 'bridge' which rests against the most resonant part of the body; and a neck with a solid surface against which the strings can be pressed and yet small enough to be encircled by the hand. Finally, at one end, logically the top, there must be some adjustable pegs for tuning the strings.

Two further considerations arise. An instrument covering the range of notes that are of practical use in music-making, from the lowest to the highest that we can comfortably hear, would need to be as big as a *double-bass*, with far more strings than one hand could comfortably manipulate and requiring some remarkable acrobatics on the part of the player. So the main stringed instruments have developed (as have wind instruments and percussion) in families: large instruments for deeper ranges, small to cover the higher.

Finally, how are the notes produced? Plucking a string produces a limited range of sound of limited resonance. It is not possible to pinpoint the first use of a *bow* in primitive music. But it seems likely, from surviving illustrations, that it was first used in Eastern countries and introduced to the West during one of the Islamic invasions. An early mention of a bow, or *kamánja*, is found in Arabic literature *c*. 900. Western examples are seen in Spanish paintings of the tenth century.

The earliest bows were shaped like the hunting bow, with an outward curving stick. The development towards many strands of horse-hair rubbed with resin and the delicate in-curving shape of the stick runs parallel with the development of the instruments. The basic requirement is for something that gives a continuous vibration to the strings by gripping them as the bow's hairs move across; thus sustaining a note as long as the bow is in contact and moving.

More art has probably been applied to the production of perfect stringed instruments than to any other family. This will raise screams of protest from addicts of the other families, but in terms of intuitive craftsmanship rather than mechanical subtleties, the statement is surely justified. It is probably quite possible that a perfect *violin* could be made of metal or glass or plastics; but the instrument-makers' art has centred around the skilful use of wood, an organic material that retains a life and beauty of its own, readily enhanced by craftsmanship. Part of the craft of violin-making has been the task of producing the lightest, thinnest and therefore the most resonant sound-box possible, while achieving quite remarkable strength in resistance to the great tension of the strings and the player's antics. The beautiful, natural-seeming shapes of string-instruments have arisen from the need for strength to resist tension – the outward curving shape being an obvious way of achieving this – and proportions and curves that help the players.

The ancestors of the violin were the *rebec* which has the pear-shaped body familiar in the mandolin; the early *fiddles* which vary in shape and size and were often, as in the case of the dancing-master's fiddle, very small, almost pocket-sized instruments of limited range and quality, and an instrument called the *lira da braccio* which came very close to the modern violin. It had five main strings, two extra untuned drone strings, or *bourdons*, and tuning pegs which would be vertical in the normal violin playing position. All these were developed in the early sixteenth century.

The *viols*, the first serious 'family' of instruments, are not as close in ancestry as the above instruments. Nevertheless they use principles that are essentially those of the violin, but with different applications. The viols had lighter, longer and less tense strings – and more of them, they had frets (fretted instruments will be dealt with later) and thinner strutted bodies. For playing they were held between the knees – hence the general term *viola da gamba*, which was most lastingly attached to the cello-sized member of the viol family which survived into the late eighteenth century – and they were bowed with the bow held above the hand rather than below as with the violin. Because of their limited expressiveness viols virtually became extinct when the violin family came to perfection, and so they never played a very important role in the development of modern orchestral music.

A cross between the viol and the violin was the *viola d'amore*. This was played like a violin, but had six or seven strings like a viol, though without frets, and a set of secondary, sympathetically vibrating strings close to the belly. It has survived as a curiosity and was even used by a composer as late as Richard Strauss (1864–1949).

It is interesting to note that instruments in which mechanics play a part, such as the harp, the piano and some percussion, have continued to develop and improve right up to the present. In contrast, the violin family was brought to remarkable perfection in Italy, notably in Cremona, by makers like Antonio Stradivari (1644–1737), at an early point in musical history. Nor, as current prices for these classic instruments indicate, have they been improved upon since, except in minor details of proportion, strength and strings. It was around 1550 that the violin achieved its recognisable shape and principles – four strings tuning in fifths – but it is difficult to pinpoint a single inventor. What we do recognise is the perfection achieved by makers like Stradivari and his near contemporaries of almost equal fame. There is so much mystique surrounding both the making and playing of violins that it is almost impossible to summarise it in a book of general intent. Was it the shape, the wood, the maturing, the varnishes, or a combination of all these things that put such splendid richness and purity into the tone of one of those incomparable treasures from Cremona? It certainly cannot be explained in scientific terms.

The bow itself has come in for as much theorising and adaptation as has the instrument. The object in making a bow is to achieve maximum lightness, strength and flexibility, so that the modern bow, like the modern instrument, is as perfect as four centuries of modification can make it.

Think of the violin as an eggshell: fragile to a sharp knock, yet enormously strong as a whole. The differences between the early violins of Cremona and the modern instruments seem slight to the casual glance, but the changes have been fundamental to the achievement of increased power and brilliance. In fact, most of the older instruments have been modified in later years to give greater flexibility of playing and added volume to their sweet but originally delicate tones. An early violin would usually have a shorter and thicker neck which was parallel to the body, the rise of the fingerboard towards the centre of the instrument being achieved by a wedge between it and the neck. The bulge of the body, both back and front, would generally be greater. As the inner strengthening was improved the violin became flatter, viewed from the side, and the neck was longer and thinner and set into the body at an angle so that the fingerboard had a natural rise. This made it easier for the stopping hand and fingers to attain the necessary positions. Accessories like the chin rest were added and developed so that the thinner violin can now easily be held in position by the chin alone, again allowing the fingers more freedom of movement.

It is the subtle variations of tone and quality achieved by the craftsman-makers through instinct and many professional secrets, that makes the violin, in particular, the subject of so much emotional discussion and writing. It is not simply a matter of sheer beauty of sound, but of the articulation of the instrument – the speed of its response to the player's actions, and the evenness of this response throughout its whole range. Some instruments are hard to play, some are easy. The great violinist Ruggiero Ricci has written: 'A Stradivari generally requires a more gentle and coaxing approach than does a Guarneri. With a Strad the note change is often more fluid. The sound of the Guarneri, on the other hand, has more core and often permits greater intensity in playing . . . The Guarneri is more often the choice of the artist who makes more excessive demands of his instrument.'

These remarks come from the sleeve-note to a fascinating LP that was issued some years ago (Brunswick AXA4521, (S) SXA4521 or MCA, still worth finding) on which Ricci played fifteen famous violins made by Stradivari, Guarneri, Andrea and Nicolo Amati, Bergonzi and Gasparo da Salò. The differences become quite obvious, even to the untrained ear, with this unique opportunity of hearing the instruments – well over a million dollars' worth of them – played one after the other.

It is not completely agreed as to whether it was the *viola* or the violin, as we know them, that came first. The earliest violas were made by Amati and Gasparo da Salò and their history is little more than a repeat of the violin's. It is the alto member of the violin family, its body length now standardised at around 41·9 cm (16½ in) as compared to the violin's 35·5 cm (14 in), and its strings are tuned a fifth lower. Comparatively few were made as demand from the composers was limited. It was not considered an essential voice in the orchestra until the beginning of the nineteenth century, although its place in the quartet was well established very much earlier. There has never been the same glamour attached to its huskier tones, and far fewer composers have been moved to write viola concertos, for there was little it could offer in the solo role that the violin could not do better. But as an additional tone colour, with a part to play that does not overlap the first or second violins or the cellos, it is now an essential voice in modern orchestration. Originally there were two sizes of viola, the smaller *contralto* and the larger *tenore* with a body of up to 48·2 cm (19 ins) in length, but the size is now standardised to the proportions mentioned above.

The bigger the body the deeper the sound – and the *violoncello* (or *cello*, as it is more usually called) is, basically, a blown-up version of the violin and viola. Its shape and proportions are in more or less direct ratio to the violin's, but its depth from front to back is comparatively much greater. The cello-maker's problems are perhaps even greater than the violin-maker's, for he must cope with much greater stresses and strains while still achieving the same egg-like strength. It is interesting to note that the indented semi-circles in the middle of the sides of the cello are not, as may appear from the position of the present-day cello-player, put there to accommodate his knees, but are shapes that have arisen in trying to achieve an even spread of sound at all pitches, as with the violin's similar indentations. In the same way, the distinctive shape of the sound-holes arose from acoustic considerations.

The *cello*, too, developed at the same time as the violin, and one of the earliest known models was made by Amati in 1572. Stradivari did not produce his first instrument until about 1680, and by this time the body length was established at sizes within a centimetre or so of 76·2 cm (30 ins). Because the cello was comparatively so resonant, it was often in danger of being passed over by some early composers in favour of the fretted bass viol or the viola da gamba, both of which were less flexible but less likely to drown the delicate tones of the violin. But gradually, as the violin became more powerful, the cello's greater flexibility won the day and it emerged as a solo instrument. The magnificent concertos written by Boccherini and Haydn and the more recently appreciated solo pieces by Bach, firmly established it as an important member of the violin family. Orchestrally it originally shared the double-bass part, but its rich contribution to the orchestral sound from Beethoven's day onward has never since been ignored. Possibly one of the greatest works ever written for the cello was Dvorak's Concerto in B Minor. 'If only I had been told that one could write a cello concerto like that!' said Brahms. Indeed, the concerto has remained the basic model for later masterpieces by such diverse composers as Elgar and Shostakovitch. The cello has been the one instrument of the violin family at which English makers have excelled.

The *double-bass*, although recognisably of the same family, had to abandon the egg-shell principle in favour of sheer strength, to cope with its long thick strings and wholehearted vibrations. Standing over 1·8 m (6 ft) high, with a body of around 1·1 m (44 ins) wide, it had to be modified simply to let a human-being get around it. The back was gradually flattened and strengthened within, the shoulders were made more sloping so that the player could get his arms round them and the join between the heavy neck and body acquired a distinctly muscular appearance. Unlike the rest of the family, the double-bass is tuned in fourths, again for the practical reason that no normal hand could stretch a fifth with the wider spacings between notes. A bass played on the higher reaches of its top string can sound remarkably like a cello, but its lower notes are essentially gruff and give some of their best effects when plucked. Indeed, a considerable part of bass technique is concerned with these *pizzicato* effects. The quite common three-string bass is used in folk and popular music for its lighter effect and singing tone.

Although the activities of the violin family have been amusingly described as 'the inside of a cat being scraped with the outside of a horse', no one would deny that it is the sheer articulate beauty of their joint and individual sounds that has made them the basis of Western orchestral music.

There are other relatives, both distant and close. The charmingly petite dancing-master's fiddles of all shapes and sizes, for example, variously known as the *pochette*, *Taschengeige* or *kit*. As the French name suggests, they were designed to be carried in the coat pocket and were used for indoor and outdoor accompaniment to dancing. Originally their shape was nearer to that of the *rebec*, but a violin shape was adopted in the late seventeenth century. The word *kit* may be an abbreviation of *cithara*, as these little instruments are much more rounded than their larger cousins. The dancing fiddle usually plays a whole octave above the normal violin; but the similar *violino piccolo* was simply a small violin tuned a fourth higher and survives today as the three-quarter size instrument often used as a starter for youngsters.

The violin is the soprano of the family and the viola the alto, and there used to be a tenor violin which was tuned a fifth below the viola. There was, however, little for it to do between the low viola and the top cello ranges and after the days of Handel and Bach it became obsolete, except as the three-quarter size cello for use by children. The true cello is the bass of the family (as distinct from the double-bass) and had its own variants in the *viola da spalla*, a small cello carried by minstrels on a shoulder strap, and the *cellone*, a larger instrument tuned a fourth lower. As if the double-bass was not impressive enough, there were various attempts, as in the *octabass* and the gigantic instrument in the Victoria and Albert Museum, to produce something for the orchestra that would correspond to the organ's deepest pipes; but the effort proved superfluous.

The *rebec*, which flourished as a medieval solo and orchestral instrument, was shaped like a half pear, the body solid except for two scooped-out boxes at either end. The top one was used as a peg-box, where the neck was a natural continuation of the solid body and the bottom one acted as a sound-box, covered with a piece of wood that had a sound-post below, two soundholes and a bridge. It was a primitive and most un-egg-like violin with a harsh tone, sometimes held in the violin position, sometimes held against the chest. It was mainly used as an accompaniment for dancing and, after it had been ousted by the violins, it went down in the world to become merely a robust thing for wandering minstrels to carry around.

4

Wind instruments

Mention of the *rebec* brings to mind the other medieval instruments with which it consorted, and thus to the early members of the wind families. Through the renewed interest in old instruments and various fascinating live and recorded performances in recent years, the names of the *shawm*, *crumhorn* and *cornett* have become newly familiar and pleasantly associated with the forthright and honest music that they played. The fashionable consort of wind instruments that was popular around 1500, and in which these instruments had an important place, was a development of the recorder family in that they exploited the vibration of reeds; an advance on simply blowing down a penny-whistle sort of instrument.

The *crumhorn* was an instrument with a cylindrical bore and a large double-reed, like the oboe, which was not actually held between the lips but blown into through a hole in the top of a cap which covered and enclosed it. This made the actual blowing similar to the recorder and protected the reed against moisture. It produced a soft, humming tone with the oboe's nasal qualities. Crumhorns varied in size, just like the recorder family. The deepest was about 91 cm (3 ft) long and the notes were obtained by opening and closing holes in the body of the instrument. The principle of a wind instrument, be it woodwind or brass, is to set up vibrations in the air, either by vibrating a reed or making the air 'bend' over an obstacle or through a shaped cup, the thickness and length of tube being used dictating the pitch of the note.

Other early wind instruments of the crumhorn type were the *sordoni* or *courtauts* and the *fagotto* which was the ancestor of the

28

bassoon. The *shawm* also used a hard double-reed. This produced a powerful sound as the reed was actually inserted in the mouth right down to its seating or 'pirouette', while the instrument was held high like a modern jazz clarinet. Various relations of the *shawm* have survived in folk and dance music, notably in the *tenora* which is heard in the Catalan coblas, or folk-dancing bands, playing the sardana sequence dances. The Macedonian *zurla* is another variant.

Alongside these reed instruments would be found the *cornett*, an interesting hybrid that was a forerunner of the brass family but which obtained its notes through the fingering of holes down its body like the woodwind, and indeed it was normally made of wood. In fact, it is just as closely related to the *shawms* and *crumhorns* as it is to its similarly named descendant the *cornet*, where only the means of blowing relates them.

The simplest of all wind instruments were those of the early pipe or flute families. The first was probably the pipe, which was simply a tube with holes cut in the sides, with the air activated by being blown past a hole and over a shaped barrier. This led to the *fife* and the *bagpipe* (whose air is supplied by filling and squeezing a bag held under the arm) and to the basic yet refined recorder family. The *recorder* is simply an elaborately and beautifully made pipe, cylindrically bored in boxwood, with a history going back to early times. Quartets of recorders were very popular during the fifteenth century, the deepest instrument then probably being the tenor; with bass instruments and beyond introduced in the middle of the sixteenth century. The consort of recorders ranged from the treble or descant instruments, through tenor to bass. These instruments are characterised by their simple, fluty sound of a very pure nature.

The extra expressiveness of the transverse-blown *flute*, as opposed to the end-blown *recorder*, led to the latter being supplanted by consorts of flutes, which survived to become the orchestral representative of the family. The keyless transverse flute developed in Eastern Europe and still survives, because the *fife* was developed as the keyed flute in comparatively recent times. The flautist blows across a hole in the side of his instrument with a not altogether attractive facial result, but is able to achieve much more fluency and subtlety than the end-blower. However, this method is less easy to control than blowing a reed; there is more danger of over-blowing, involuntarily invoking the principle that a harder blow produces a note an octave higher – which, of course, applies to all wind instruments to some extent.

The flute is not always made of wood, but often of metal. This is usually the case with its smaller brother, the *piccolo*. Metal instruments allow the maker's art full flow by way of engravings and other embellishments.

The main advance in woodwind instruments, which still employ the basic, primitive means of producing sounds that have remained unchanged over the centuries, has been in the refinement and sophistication of the means of producing the various notes. The simple expedient of closing and opening holes by the application and removal of the thumb and finger tips works well enough on small instruments, like the higher pitched recorders or the *ocarina*, but becomes impracticable in larger instruments or those designed to play through a range of several octaves.

Serious developments in the mechanics of wind instruments only came during the Haydn-Mozart-Beethoven years of the eighteenth and early nineteenth centuries. First, simple 'keys' were added: a basic brass lever rotating on a pin with a leather pad at one end which fell over the rimless hole. As the lever was depressed at one end the pad was raised, to be returned by a somewhat sluggish flat brass spring when the lever was released. They were neither precise in action nor totally efficient hermetically. The more of these an instrument had the less efficient it became, as more air escaped and faults developed.

The need for remote control of the more distant keys by rods therefore became essential, and the pivoting, springing and materials were gradually improved. Once a thoroughly efficient mechanical system was evolved more scientifically accurate placement of the holes was sought. Mid-nineteenth-century manufacturers like Albert and Sax perfected the basic, present-day 'simple system' which is still adhered to by some players and nations. Further innovations were introduced by Theobald Boehm (1794–1881) and his system became the leading rival to the simple system, first with regard to the clarinet, then to the flute and the other instruments. Without going into the complications of Boehm's researches, it is sufficient to state that he devised new fingerings based on the use of ring keys which allowed the finger not only to close the hole under it but, by pressing a ring attached to a rod, to close other distant keys at the same time. It was Boehm's fingering that caused more controversy than his valuable acoustic discoveries which involved using bigger holes and different bores and did much to purify and empower the tones of the principal wind instruments. But it was not until well into the twentieth century that the Boehm system became the universal standard for flutes, clarinets, oboes, bassoons and saxophones, with many diehards standing out against it in favour of the so-called 'simple' system until the last possible moment.

There are no more attractive wind instruments than some of the decorated silver flutes. The reed instruments, however, ended up by being more functional than beautiful, the basic shape of the instrument more or less hidden by a complicated fuzz of keys, rods and levers – like a building covered with scaffolding.

The *clarinet* was an 'invented' instrument; the brainchild of one J. C. Denner (1655–1707), an instrument-maker of Nuremberg. Its novelty is the use of the single reed fastened in a groove in the mouthpiece, which leads to its claim to be the first instrument with the reed completely controlled by the lips. The *chalumeau* is generally regarded as the ancestor of the clarinet. It was a small instrument of some 20 cm (8 ins) in length, and it was while experimenting with this that Denner may have hit upon the principles of his clarinet. The *embouchure* (the way the mouth is placed over the mouthpiece and reed) for the clarinet is still varied. The mouthpiece can be turned, so the instrument can either be played with the reed uppermost or underneath, controlled by either top or lower lip. The German method of playing with the reed downwards appeared to be most effective and is the method most widely used today.

By virtue of their similar natures and fingering, the clarinetist can switch to the less common *bass-clarinet*, an attractive instrument whose extra length is curled up into a shape made familiar through the saxophone family, and the *basset-horn*, which was originally a curved

31

tenor version of the clarinet. Its present form as a straight instrument with upturned bell, was invented around 1770 in Bavaria. It has a deeper and more sombre tone than the clarinet. Although it has not survived as a regular member of the orchestra, it is occasionally called upon for special effects by adventurous composers like Richard Strauss, and there is one delightful duet for clarinet and basset-horn written by Mendelssohn which Jack Brymer has recorded.

The *oboe* uses the principle of the double-reed (which is usually made from a single long reed bent double with its doubled end pared down until it divides) employed by the much earlier shawm. The oboe is the central instrument of the woodwind sections of the orchestra, as the violin is of the strings. It made its first appearance in a recognizable modern form around 1660, thus preceding the clarinet by about half a century. Its advances on the shawm were due to it being manufactured in three separate pieces (as the clarinet is) which allowed it to be bored with greater accuracy. This, together with its narrower bore, a narrower reed and smaller bell, toned down the shawm's raucous qualities to something more suited to eventual use in a classical orchestra. Originally known in England as the French *hoboy* or *hautbois*, it managed to become the principal wind voice of the orchestra within a hundred years of its inception. Its developments then were parallel with those of the clarinet, eventually succumbing to the Boehm system and modern perfecting of its mechanism. The beautifully plaintive tone of the oboe changes, when angry, to a sharp quack, reminding us of its shawmly ancestry.

The nearest relative of the shawm in use today is the curiously named *cor anglais*, the *anglais* or *inglese* apparently arising from the Europeans' amused recognition of the quiet-spoken qualities of the English language. It is, in fact, a tenor oboe or *oboe da caccia*, with softer and deeper tones, distinguished in appearance by its globular bell or occasionally flared horn. Another deceased ancestor was the *oboe d'amore* which was pitched a minor third below the oboe.

The other prominent member of the woodwind family in regular use today is the *bassoon* (in German and Italian the *fagott* or *fagotto* – a name which emphasises its likeness to a bundle of sticks tied together) which comes from a prolific family. In the seventeenth century there were as many as five varieties in regular use, with quaint names like *dolcian*, *fagottino*, *tenoroon* and *quint-bassoon*, covering all ranges of the musical scale. The standard bassoon which survives is often thought of as a bass oboe, its total range being two octaves below, but these lower notes are not included in its natural range. In its higher ranges it can be a gracefully melodic instrument, far removed from the comic buffoon so often asked to pump away on its lower notes with humorous intent.

Like the oboe it is a double-reed instrument and is usually made of maple or rosewood, dividing into five sections. The total length of tubing is around 2·6 m (102 ins), the doubling of the tube reducing its actual length to around a manageable 1·2 m (4 ft). Until the eighteenth century, the equivalent of the modern bassoon would have been used mainly as a bass instrument with its now defunct relatives used for higher parts, but gradually it became better appreciated for its mixture of richness and flexibility. Bach first wrote for the bassoon around 1708.

The double or *contra-bassoon*, an octave lower in pitch, is certainly of a more portly nature and is mainly used as a substitute for a string bass in woodwind works or, sparingly like the tuba, for extra orchestral richness.

The interest of a detailed study of woodwind instruments is in seeing how the purest and most functional designs – the modern oboe, clarinet and bassoon – survived, with the more cumbersome and less graciously sounding relatives falling by the wayside and later eccentric members of the family failing as usurpers. The bassoon survived its close relatives, the shawms, bombards and pommers, and elbowed aside quirkish rivals like the *bassonore* – a metal bassoon primarily intended for use in military bands.

One instrument that managed to survive in limited use was the *heckelphone*, perfected in 1904 by the German Heckel family. Looking rather like a cor anglais, it has a bore double the size of the standard oboe and plays the role of a baritone oboe. It requires a reed of bassoon proportions and provides a rich voice lying between the oboes and bassoons. Richard Strauss was one of the first composers to use it effectively.

There are, of course, other, rather curious wind instruments that were designed for specific purposes, for instance that very specialised outsider, the *bagpipe*. This is an instrument not intended for orchestral use, except in consort with its own kind, but specifically intended as an accompaniment to marching and dancing. The basic thought behind the bagpipe is the ingenious idea of building up a reservoir of air in a bag, ideally made of sheep's or goat's bladder or skin, which is air-tight and absorbent. The air is then economically forced through the reed pipes when the bag is compressed by the player's arm. The player maintains the necessary head of air and is able to keep up his efforts for a considerable period while on the move.

Early bagpipes were of a simple nature: an intake pipe with a non-return valve, bag, and the outlet pipe, or chanter, with a reed and finger holes. The now characteristic second pipe, or drone, which provides a continuous note, was added later, no doubt to produce a music of primitive savagery that would suitably alarm the bagpiping force's opponents. The elaborate modern Scottish bagpipe can have as many as six drones to widen the range of keys in which the music may be played. The chanter generally has a double reed like the oboe, the drones usually have thinner single or beating reeds. The French equivalent, the *musette*, generally has double reeds throughout.

Primitive British bagpipes have been made from many types of skin and various native woods, but, in general, harder woods like ebony which are less susceptible to damp, or even ivory or plastic, are now used. The Scottish bagpipes are of various kinds, the one we know best being the elaborate and decorative Highland pipe, the *piob mhor*, which has become the predominant military instrument. The oldest surviving instrument of this kind dates back to almost 1400. Other kinds, like the lowland instrument, were activated by bellows and were used mainly for dance accompaniment with the player seated. The Irish military bagpipe is more or less the same as the Scottish, but with slight modifications. The only surviving English bagpipe is the Northumbrian.

From the bagpipes we move to a group of instruments where the bellows principle was developed to activate a number of tuned free-reeds. The *accordion* and *concertina* were both originated around 1829.

Straps on the round, square or, in the case of the concertina, hexagonal endboards through which the hands pass, enable the player to support the instrument and control the keys opening valves at one or both ends. In between the two ends are the compressible bellows, drawing in air as they are expanded by the action of the player's arms and forcing it out as they are compressed. The concertina's reeds originally produced one note on compression and another on expansion, like the mouth-blown *harmonica* or *mouth-organ*, which makes it less practical to play. The concertina patented by Sir Charles Wheatstone, was designed to produce one note for both actions of the bellows and thus became a more straightforward instrument to play. The principle was adopted in the modern piano-accordion, which provides the player with a piano-type keyboard to operate the valves and reeds and give maximum flexibility.

5

Brass

instruments

The *saxophone*, a comparatively modern invention, is one of the newest members of the brass family. These hybrid instruments, using brass or metal bodies but employing the reeds and fingerings of the woodwind family, were invented by Adolph Sax in 1846. It was his experiments with metal clarinets that led to their perfection. With a very wide conical bore they could offer a louder, fuller sound able to compete with the brass in military bands and so on, combined with the flexibility of the woodwind technique. The members of the family in common use now are the alto, tenor, baritone and bass saxophones; while the straight, clarinet-like soprano, which is very difficult to play in tune, has an occasional revival.

As it turned out, although the saxophones did take their due place in the military band, they became most familiar in jazz and its later developments, their rather sexy tones ideally suited to the sentiments of popular music. They use a single, thickish reed and produce a powerful sound which competes adequately against the trumpets and trombones used in force in the modern swing orchestra. The now familiar S-shape was contrived, like most instrumental shapings, to reduce the considerable length of tubing to a manoeuvrable size.

It is perhaps this shape that leads the eye, if not the ear, directly to the world of early 'brass' instruments, perhaps to the *serpent*. This strange contraption, so aptly named with its several wriggles, was made of wood, often leather-covered, with a cup-shaped mouthpiece leading by way of a brass crook to the long conical body some 2·4 m (8 ft) in length as the worm travels. The notes were simply produced by opening and closing six large fingerholes. It came from a prolific family, some of them dressed up to look like real serpents or dragons, which gloried in such fine names as *hibernicon, serpentcleide, serpent piffault, serpent froveille, ophibaryton, ophimonocleide* and *Russian bassoon.*

These instruments introduce us to sounds produced by yet another basic means. Instead of a reed being vibrated to produce amplified vibrations in the bore, the principle in the brass instruments is to produce the initial vibration with the lips, amplifying this by first producing it in the small cup of the mouthpiece, forcing it through a narrow aperture into the very much larger conical bores of the instruments and amplifying it down the considerable length of tubing necessitated by the feebler source. The simplest of such instruments is the *long horn*, originally probably a ram's horn, either straight or with a slight curvature at the end like the *alphorn*. These, like the *bugle*, which is simply a straight horn rolled up into a compact shape, are capable of producing a note. Furthermore, loosening or tightening the lips, and blowing harder or softer to various degrees, produces its octaves and its natural harmonics, that is, C, E and G (in the key of C), which are the notes that make up a typical bugle call. The basic note depends on the length of the tube, and advances in brass instruments (generally made of that malleable metal which gave them their name) came in the various means employed to vary this length temporarily, so producing other notes and their corresponding octaves and harmonics.

One way of doing it was developed in the *sackbut*, which in its modern form, the *trombone*, has seen less change than most instruments. In the former, one U-shaped tube slid over the arms of another U-shaped tube of lesser dimensions. Thus the overall length of the tube could be simply and quite easily extended with one arm and hand, while the other held the instrument to the lips. In this case, the note had to be found by ear, moving the slide to the right position, rather as a string player must find his notes by custom on a non-fretted instrument. In some of the earliest instruments working on the trombone principle, the *trompettes de ménestrels*, the principle was there in cruder form, with the whole body of the instrument being slid along the extended tube of the mouthpiece. In the subsequent *sacqueboute*, or *sackbut* (German, *posaune*), the principle of the looped slide with a double piston action meant that the slide only had to be moved half the distance, thus giving extra mobility and stability. The trombone used around 1500 was very much the same as it is today, which is quite a remarkable example of early perfection.

All the brass instruments are fundamentally the same, involving a cupped mouthpiece and a considerable length of conical tubing ending in a flared bell. The only differences are in the width and length of the tubing (the principle of the bigger the deeper being the same in any instrument) and in the shape into which they are conveniently twisted.

The ungarnished tubes of the early 'natural' instruments meant, of course, that they could only play in one key, although the pitch could be altered slightly by various physical contortions of the lips. Not only are these difficult for the player, but they do not produce a very pure result. The pitch of such instruments could be altered unscientifically by the insertion of the hand in the bell, a device still used in horn playing. A scientific alteration of pitch could only be achieved by altering the length of the tubing.

The first advancement in brass playing was made by diverting the air-stream through added lengths of tubing, or crooks, which could be supplied in unlimited variety. But the instrument could still only be played in one key with the notes limited to the harmonics and whatever else the player could contrive. Up to the time of Haydn, most pieces involving brass were written in B♭ or E♭, keys natural to the instrument, and the parts remained fairly unambitious. Up to this time there were various experiments to allow these additional crooks to slide and it is conceivable that all brass instruments might have ended up as larger or smaller variants of the trombone. However, the means for further advance came with the invention of the valve around 1815.

The principle of the valve system is again quite simple. The basic tubing is supplied with three alternative loops through which the air can pass. In the natural position these loops are closed off by a valve or piston. There is a hole in the body of the valve and when depressed by a finger this coincides with the bore of the loop and allows the air through the extra length of tubing. In the simplest form, the first valve opens a loop which adds an extra eighth to the length of the total tubing and lowers its pitch by a whole tone; the second valve opens a loop that lowers the pitch by half a tone; while a third valve opens a loop that lowers the pitch by one and a half tones. This last could also be achieved by opening the first and second valves together, of course, but the extra valve adds to the flexibility of the instrument. These valves, together with the number of notes that can be played in any one position, allow every note of the chromatic scale to be obtained, thus putting the brass on an equal footing with all the other orchestral instruments. The rest was simply a matter of establishing the ideal pitch for each instrument and the most functional shape. Curiously, the trombone remained the one instrument to keep to the sliding system, although valve trombones have been made and used. This means that one instrument in the family can still play a true glissando, from the lowest note achievable in any lip position to the highest, passing through every degree of the scale on the way. This pleasant sound is occasionally employed in orchestral music but has found its most lucrative outlet in jazz, where a well-timed trombone glissando supplies a special thrill for the connoisseur.

Each instrument in the family achieved a standard size and shape, the B♭ *trumpet*, for example, becoming the norm, but with higher *clarino* instruments (as written for by Bach) and lower ones being developed for special purposes. The trumpet was so designed to produce a clear, sharp, fairly piercing range of sounds. The *cornet*, with a wider bore and shorter length, was designed to produce a fatter, mellower tone. The trombones added their own mixture of gruffness or mellowness to the orchestral palette. The natural instruments, like the bugle, *posthorn* and alphorn, have survived for their own special uses in military, ceremonial and folk music.

The unique qualities of the horn, distant and mysterious, arise basically from an exceptional length of narrow bore tubing which makes it physically the most difficult to play with pure and accurate results. It was the horn, therefore, that caused the most trouble and which went through the most complicated series of improvements and modifications before the ideal orchestral instrument was evolved as late as 1899. Technically referred to as the double horn, it took the best characteristics of earlier instruments in F and in B♭ and with an extra valve enabled the player to shift immediately from either of these. It was the general adoption of the French model, with its comparatively small bore, rather than the German model with its larger bore and somewhat coarser sound, that led to the name of *French horn* being generally used, although, to be fair, many of its principal advances came from German manufacturers and inventors. It would be clearer, perhaps, to concentrate on its shape more and refer to the coiled instrument, with which we are most familiar nowadays, as the *helical* horn, simply differentiating between these and the lingering straight ones.

Also in the brass family are a whole range of instruments that can be loosely classified as *key bugles* and which were developed mainly for military and, to a large extent, marching purposes. For considerations of convenience and sound quality it is not really ideal to have the bell of any brass instrument pointing forwards and, because of the human shape, partly downwards. It is certainly not nice for the person in front, as anyone who has to sit in front of the trombone section in an orchestra will appreciate! It was a fairly natural development, then, that a whole range of brass instruments, developing from the bugle, should be made with their bells pointing upwards and their bulky bodies capable of being hugged in the arms of the person who had to carry them. The *ophicleide*, a brass bugle-cum-horn, was invented around 1817 and had its heyday between 1830 and 1890. It helped out the trombone section with its weighty sound, but was eventually replaced by the *tuba*, the largest of the heaven-directed bugle family.

With the final sophistication of the valve (which generally lowered the tone but could also be contrived to raise it), a full range of instruments for military band use was developed to cover the whole usable scale. The cornet lingers as a compromise between forward and up-pointing families, its slightly vulgar tones finding favour in brass and military bands but losing out to the trumpet in orchestral and jazz circles. The modern instruments of the marching kind are the *tenor horn, baritone, euphonium, bass* or *bombardon*. In addition, there are the big orchestral *tuba*, the even bigger *Wagner tuba* and the marching tuba which coils sexily around the player and is generally known as the *sousaphone*. To lump all these together is perhaps a little misleading – the *Wagner tuba*, for example, is not a pure tuba but a cross between a horn and a *saxhorn*. The latter, an invention of the indefatigable Mr Sax (already noted for his saxophones), differ from the existing bugle family only in possessing an improved valve and a uniformity of styling which make them a co-ordinated family. The saxhorns had a period of popularity, much promoted by the famous Distin family, but never managed to supplant the already well-developed instruments of a similar nature established by other makers. A kind of bass ophicleide, the *bombardon*, introduced by the same firm who tried to promote a *valve-trombone*, also had a limited reign.

But, despite all the permutations and variations in this family of instruments, the basic established shapes will be familiar to most people and, as with the woodwind and string groups, part of the pleasure that these instruments give is in the aesthetic appreciation of their convolutions, mainly dictated by nature and only partly by man's often misplaced ingenuity.

Before leaving the wind instruments, the *mute* must be mentioned. The mutes used on stringed instruments are simply a kind of clamp pushed onto the bridge between the strings to dampen down the vibrations and thus produce a quieter, muted and subtly altered tone. Mutes are used in connection with woodwind, but generally all the control required can be obtained by the player.

For the brass, particularly trumpets and trombones, the mute is more frequently used. Basically it is a hollow cone which is put into the bell of the instrument to make the sound take a more devious route to the exit, achieving in the 'straight' mute a softening of the natural brassy tone. Applied sophistication in the playing of trombones and trumpets, particularly as developed in popular music (one immediately thinks of the silky soft tone that trombonist Tommy Dorsey achieved), to some extent makes the mute unnecessary, but it can be splendidly used for special effects. The wow-wow mute, which has a flat end over which the open hand can be placed and removed to produce an alternating open and shut tone, has been used with great effect. Similar effects can be achieved by inserting and removing other mutes, or waving a bowler hat-like 'derby' mute in front of the bell.

6

Keyboard instruments

There can be no particular logic in moving from one group of instruments to another. It is simply their importance that leads us next to the intriguing and complicated keyboard instruments. The basic principle of these takes us back to the principle of the *harp* – a considerable number of tuned strings on a permanent frame. The harp depends on the dexterity of the player's fingers to put the strings into operation and, because of the impossibility of handling one string for every note of several chromatic octaves, the harp manufacturers resorted to some very complicated devices for limiting the necessary number of strings. But if a series of levers or keys could be devised that lay more easily under the hands and which, when depressed, operated mechanism that either plucked or hit the strings and, moreover, the instrument could be made to stand, so to speak, on its own feet – well, thoughts like these must have occurred to the early pioneers of keyboard instruments. The aesthetic, decorative possibilities of keyboard instruments became important very early in their history, simply because they could not be put away in a cupboard. As well as being musical instruments, they had to be pieces of furniture. Seeing a group of keyboard instruments in a museum one is impressed by the intricate craftsmanship and affection that has gone into their outward appearance. Indeed, this skill is sometimes even more remarkable than the weak noise that comes out of many of the earlier models.

The actual keyboard, with its now familiar grouping of black-and-white notes, seems to have been a bit of musical logic that was adopted right from the beginning, a direct interpretation of the

43

characteristics of a major scale with its fixed order of tones and half-tones. The important developments over the centuries were to be first, the improved means of tensioning the strings and getting the best sound out of them, and second, the improvement of the action (the mechanism that lies between the key which the finger strikes and the part which actually produces a sound from the string).

From this last point of view, keyboard instruments fall into two groups: those which use a plucking mechanism, and those in which the strings are struck by some kind of hammer. The main plucked instruments are the *harpsichord*, the *virginals* and the *spinet*. In all these the operative unit is the 'jack'. This is a piece of hard wood of about 15·2 cm (6 ins), although it can be more or less, standing upright with its pointed top level with the string. The action pushes this up past the string which is then caught or plucked by a small pivoted 'tongue' which remains rigid while it plucks but is knocked back into a slot as the jack falls. This is putting it in its simplest form. The matter is complicated by the fact that the most elaborate harpsichords have at least three sets of strings; two tuned in unison as in the piano and at the normal piano 8-foot pitch and one tuned an octave higher at 4-foot pitch. There are simpler harpsichords with one keyboard and one set of strings, but the larger, more developed instrument has two keyboards and as many as four or five strings to each key brought in and out of action by stops and pedals, so that such harpsichords, by fairly complicated means, can achieve various tones and a varied range. In addition, the mechanism of all keyboard instruments must include a means of damping the strings, that is, a way of cutting off the vibrations once the string has been struck or plucked, plus a means of taking the dampers out of action when a sustained sound is required. The occasional, big eighteenth-century harpsichord with an additional set of 16-foot pitch strings was quite a formidable instrument. A means of coupling, or playing more than one set of strings together, was a later development.

The permutations are endless. The *harpsichord* originated in Italy and models survive from the early sixteenth century. Generally plain and elegant, they were made of cypress wood, although often enclosed in an extra case, exquisitely decorated to suit an elegant home. Their clear but weak tones blended well with voices and were sufficient for continuo playing. Many of the ensuing advances in harpsichord-making took place in the Low Countries and famous Antwerp makers, like Ruckers and Andries, were probably responsible for the introduction of the second keyboard. Other countries at first imported Italian or Flemish instruments, but by the mid-eighteenth century foreign makers like Kirckman had settled in London, and Germany had its own flourishing industry.

The harpsichord, like the grand piano, developed as a solo instrument, becoming larger and more expensive. If the harpsichord was, to a great extent, pushed aside by the even more flexible piano, it never ceased to exist as an instrument with different and irreplaceable characteristics, ideal for certain kinds of music. Although the harpsichord advocate will not agree that the harpsichord limits itself by its lack of a graded touch, there is less control over a jack than a hammer, but a good player can achieve a high degree of control and a sensitivity to the feel of the tongue on the string. Where the piano was to gain favour was in competition with the bigger orchestra.

The harpsichord-makers were largely responsible for the manufacture of other similar instruments. These were the domestic equivalent of the harpsichord which had become the equivalent of the grand piano. The *virginals* was a smaller oblong instrument of a rather less ambitious nature. It should be noted, however, that the name 'virginal' was often used in England to include all the plucked instruments. The *spinet* was a virginal that reverted to the grand piano shape or else was nearly triangular, a kind of 'baby grand' of the plucked keyboard family.

The history of the piano-type instrument in which the strings are struck was not, as it might seem, just a sequel to the plucked instrument. Its development was not only roughly parallel, but actually goes much further back in the shape of the *clavichord*. In principle it could be said to go right back to an instrument built by Pythagoras which he called the *monochord*. This consisted of a single string which could be shortened by a movable bridge to produce the fundamental notes of the existing scales when struck with a small hammer. Thenceforth the *clavichord* or *clavicordium* appears in musical history, in many and varied forms. By the early fifteenth century there were certainly instruments with ten or more tuned strings and a chromatic keyboard. By the time of the earliest surviving instruments, around the mid-sixteenth century, its range had been increased to four octaves and by the early seventeenth century a variety of music was being written especially for it. The strings were struck by a light blade or 'tangent' which travelled a short distance to rest against the string until the key was released. The tone was clear and had a delicate beauty of its own, but was essentially weak. In many of the early keyboard instruments it is interesting to note that it was sometimes the practice to add to their limited number of octaves a few lower fundamental notes for strength in the bass.

The notion of the pianoforte, that is a keyboard instrument that could be played both softly (*piano*) and loudly (*forte*), may have long fermented in various ingenious minds. But such an instrument really required a striking action which allowed for a more easily graded touch than a plucking one. Around the beginning of the seventeenth century the desire grew for an instrument that could combine the delicacy and expressiveness of the clavichord with the power and brilliance of the harpsichord. The French composer Couperin clearly expressed this desire when he wrote in 1713: 'The harpsichord is perfect as to compass, and brilliant in itself, but as it is impossible to swell or diminish the volume of sound I shall always feel grateful to anyone who, by the exercise of infinite art supported by fine taste, contrives to render this instrument capable of expression.'

In fact, Bartolomeo Cristofori, who is generally credited as the pioneer of the *piano e forte*, had, right at the beginning of the eighteenth century, devised that part of the piano action which was to be called the *escapement* and which was to be fundamental to the development of the modern instrument. This arrangement of levers and springs, only subtly improved in the present day models, allowed the hammer to fall back into place immediately it had struck the string (unlike the clavichord tangent), at the same time making a damper fall against the string to cut off its vibrations. This we might call the basic action. The so-called loud and soft pedals do not actually increase or decrease the volume, which the player controls by the force with which he depresses the key, but they cut off or sustain the note. The 'soft' pedal either shortens the hammers' distance of travel or holds the dampers against the strings so long as it is in use or limits the hammers' application to only one string of two or three; the 'loud' pedal keeps the dampers away from the strings and is more correctly called the sustaining pedal, as it allows the note to continue sounding.

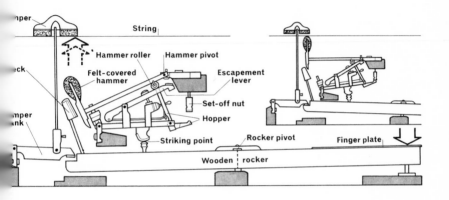

EXAMPLE OF A GRAND PIANO ACTION

Cristofori's experiments were continued by Gottfried Silbermann, but both met with a certain lack of support from the musical world. The great Bach, a dedicated harpsichord man, found the new *piano* weak in the treble and heavy to the touch. Gradually, however, the composers were won over to the piano. In London, now a centre of harpsichord manufacture, one of Bach's sons, Johann Christian, became a great champion of the *pianoforte*, and in Austria Mozart was one of the first major composers to be won over entirely by the possibilities of the new instrument. In London, one of Silbermann's pupils, Zumpe, introduced his famous 'square' piano. These earlier instruments, now often referred to as '*fortepianos*', had certain fundamental failings: a slowness of action (which was often, however, quite light); a hardness of tone caused by the hammers generally

47

being leather-covered; a limited volume arising from the difficulty of tensioning the strings on the wooden frames; and a range limited by the length of string possible.

The *grand piano* came in around 1772. The famous Broadwood model, with its patented pedals, was introduced in 1783. The first metal frame received its patent in 1825. When one realises that the total pull on the frame of a modern grand is around thirty tons the importance of a frame of permanent shape and strength can be appreciated. It was as late as 1850 that felt was generally adopted as the ideal material with which to cover the hammers, although various other materials had their supporters for a much longer period.

The full-size grand is only a domestic instrument for those with wallets and houses large enough to cope with its price and size. The great advance in the domestic upright piano came with the development of overstringing. This method uses an advanced frame in which greater lengths of string could be used by putting them diagonally, one behind the other, in a double set.

The variety of pianos is astonishing. If it has found its ideal and consummation in the elegant concert grand, it has possibly attracted more cranks than any other instrument – this, of course, is its fascination. In most cases the odd shapes have arisen in an attempt to improve its sound. But, fortunately for our delight, the outward aspect has also attracted considerable artistic ingenuity, especially in those leisured days of the nineteenth century when time could be spent on the more decorative aspects of instruments. At the same time, an interesting economic reflection of the times is to be found in advertisements for functional 'cottage' pianos and front-parlour instruments with prices ranging from the twelve guinea (£12.60) mark.

1. *Top* Conch shells were probably among the earliest natural wind instruments and were part of Babylonian music-making *c.* 1000 BC. This shell has a brass mouthpiece, sounds two notes and is of Tibetan origin. *Bottom* The cowhorn, another natural object put to musical use, was used particularly as a war horn up to the early Middle Ages. This modern instrument is brass-mounted at the bell and centre and is end-blown.

2. The beautiful shape of the Irish harp is well-known from its inclusion in the Royal arms. Smaller and more portable than the modern instrument, most of the surviving old models date from around 1700.

3. Although maintaining the traditional shape, the modern pedal-action harp is a large and complicated instrument, often elaborately decorated, over 1.8m (6ft) high and of considerable weight.

4. The viols, a family of
bowed string instruments
dominated European music
from the fifteenth to the
seventeenth centuries, but
were gradually ousted by
the violin family. The one
at left was made by Peter
Wamsley at the 'Heart and
Hautboy', Pickadilly, London', c. 1750. 5. The bass
viola da gamba was the
longest surviving member
of the viol family and was
used as a solo instrument
well into the eighteenth
century. This one was
manufactured by Henry
Jay of Southwark in 1613

6. The viola d'amore, a type of treble viol with a secondary set of vibrating 'sympathetic strings', had a plain fingerboard and was played like a violin. This is an eighteenth century instrument.

7. The violin family gradually superseded the viols and now form the basis of the modern orchestra. This grouping of violin, viola, cello and double-bass shows their comparative sizes.

8.   The viola is the alto instrument of the violin family, of similar proportions to the violin but a fifth larger in size and tuned a fifth lower.

9. The violin was brought to perfection in Italy from the sixteenth to eighteenth centuries. Some changes in proportions have been made subsequently as a comparison of this model, made by J. C. Ficker, Neukirschen Bey Adorf, *c.* 1750, and the modern instrument opposite shows.

Changes in modern violins have naturally been in the interest of greater flexibility and fuller tone. The length and angle of fingerboard and body proportions have undergone subtle alterations.

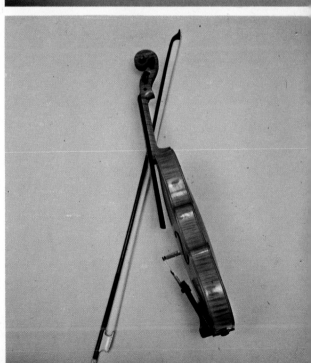

11. The violoncello, usually called the cello, is the bass instrument of the violin family, with its lowest string tuned an octave below the lowest string of the viola. It is played in a seated position between the knees.

Cello

12. This beautifully decorated cello was made by William Foster Jr, *c.* 1790. It was owned by George IV when he was Prince of Wales, and bears his crest.

13. The double-bass is the largest member of the violin family and still shows some characteristics of the viols. It is heavily built and is played in the standing position with considerable use of pizzicato.

and 15. Apart from
the standard violins, in-
struments of various shapes
and sizes were used in folk
music, especially as an
accompaniment to dancing.
The fiddle (*bottom*) made
by John Walsh 'over ganst
the Talbot Inne' London
1766 and the kit (*top*) *c.*
1750–6, are examples.

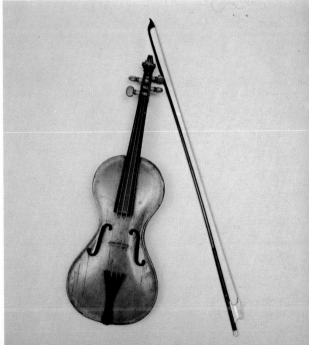

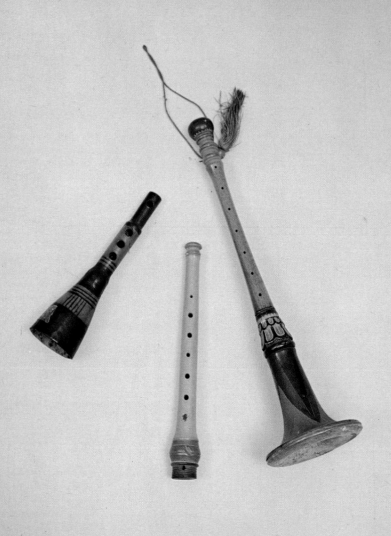

16. Three instruments of the shawm family in current use. *Left:* Ailgarita from Nigeria or Camerons with 4 holes, wood covered with leather. *Centre:* Sopel from Dalmatia, boxwood with 6 holes. *Right:* Chirimia from Central America, of turned wood with brightly painted bell and 7 holes.

17. The history of the recorder family goes back to the twelfth century. The modern instruments, based on seventeenth and eighteenth century designs (when it was known as the English flute), are made of ebonite or wood.

18. The clarinet is a single-reed instrument used in both classical music and jazz. The body is generally of wood or ebonite, but is sometimes of metal. The group here includes the bass-clarinet with its upturned bell and bent mouthpiece.

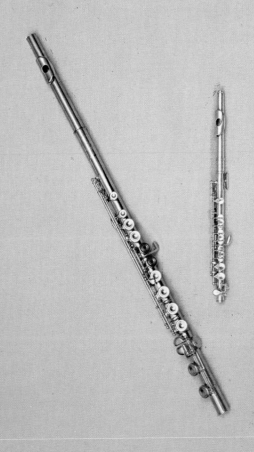

19. The modern flute and the smaller piccolo are technical developments of various kinds of early pipes. Early flutes were end-blown; the modern instrument is side-blown. The ones here are made of nickel-silver.

20. A modern clarinet (*left*) contrasted with an old instrument made in boxwood and ivory by Key of Charing Cross *c.* 1800.

21.   The oboe, based on instruments of considerable antiquity, is the leading voice of the woodwind section. It is made of wood and has a double reed. The cor anglais is a longer and lower-toned kind of oboe with a distinctive bulbous bell.

22. The bassoon, a double reed instrument, is really a bass oboe with a tube of such length (about 2.7m or 9ft) that it has to be doubled back on itself for easier handling. There is also a contra-bassoon of twice the size.

23. The basset horn is really a tenor clarinet, similar in appearance to the bass-clarinet with upturned bell and bent crook to the mouthpiece. This one, made by Pask of the Lowther Arcade in nickel silver, once belonged to the English clarinet-ist Henry Lazarus (1815–95).

24. Bagpipes, which are basically sets of pipes with some kind of air reservoir, come in all shapes and sizes according to their country or district of origin. This is the familiar modern Scottish instrument.

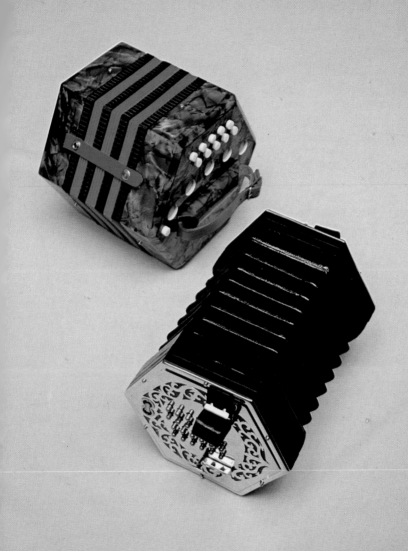

25. The concertina is very much a folk instrument and varies considerably in shape and size. These two contemporary instruments are made by Scarf.

26.   The accordion developed from an instrument similar to the concertina, latterly best-known in its keyboard form, the piano accordion, frequently of German origin as is this modern instrument by Horch.

27. The saxophone was created by Adolph Sax in the mid-nineteenth century and intended mainly for military band use, combining brass sonority with wood-wind flexibility. They have become very much jazz instruments. These are bass, alto and soprano saxes.

28. The tenor-saxophone has established itself as the most popular of these instruments, particularly in the jazz field. This and the preceding instruments are modern saxes in nickel-plated brass.

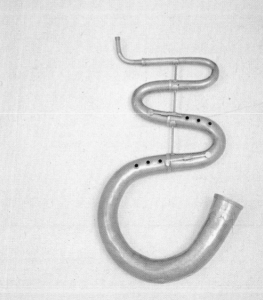

. The cornett (cornet-
o in this case) was an
trument with brass type
outhpiece and fingered
les which has gone out of
neral use. This is either
mid-eighteenth century
odel, or possibly a copy
unknown make. The
ooden body is covered
th black leather.

,0. The serpent is simi-
ar in principal with its
ong body bent into the
hape which suggested the
ame. Although usually of
vood, this early nineteenth-
century model is of copper
and made in four sections.

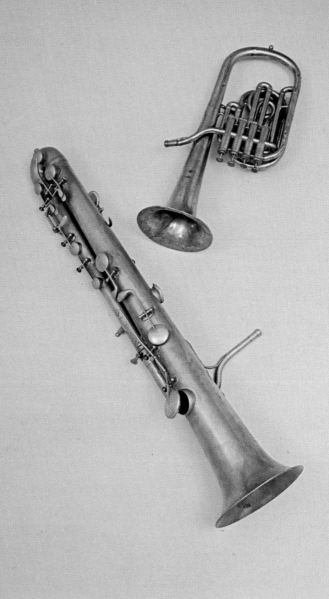

31. (*Left*) The ophicleide was never a particularly serious instrument but had some vogue in Victorian days. This one is made in nickel silver. (*Right*) The saxhorns, a family of brass instruments, are still used. This one is an E♭ alto instrument made in Paris and has perinet valves and tuning slide.

2 and 33. The trumpet nd cornet (a shorter intrument with wider bore) re keyed developments of he simple bugle or horn. Jsed orchestrally, they are articularly prominent in rass, military band and azz circles.

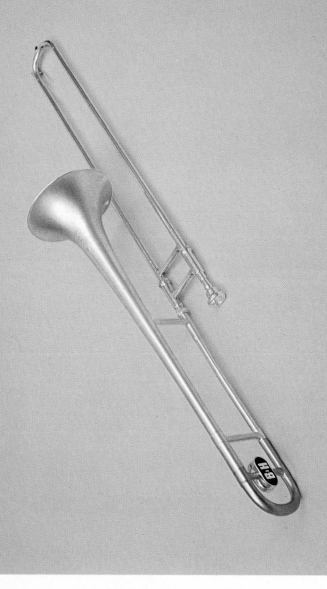

34. The trombone has remained virtually unchanged since its early days when it was known as the sackbut. It is now the only brass instrument that lengthens its tubes solely by means of a slide.

35. Various brass instruments have been developed, often with marching band use in mind. This family group shows the tuba, euphonium and tenor-horn.

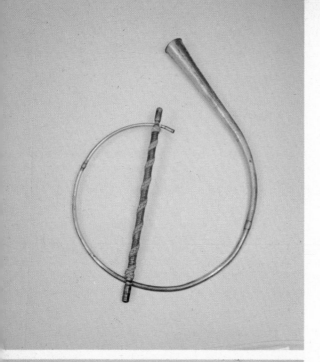

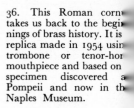

36. This Roman corn·
takes us back to the begi·
nings of brass history. It is
replica made in 1954 usin·
trombone or tenor-ho·
mouthpiece and based on
specimen discovered a·
Pompeii and now in th·
Naples Museum.

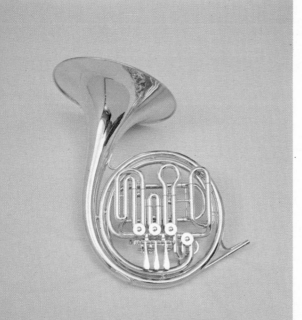

37. The modern French
horn is the sophisticated
development of various
kinds of horns, straight and
coiled.

38. The spinet was an early keyboard instrument with the strings plucked by jacks on the same principal as the harpsichord. It was in vogue in England in the seventeenth and eighteenth centuries.

39. The virginals was a sort of household version of the spinet or harpsichord, small and portable and much favoured as a lady's instrument. This English instrument was made by Robert Hartley in 1664.

40. The harpsichord illustrated is a double-manual instrument built by John Broadwood in 1799. It has a mahogany case with brass fittings. Recently rebuilt, with nylon jacks and 'quill-tone', its current value would be around £6,500.

41. The clavichord was an ancestor of the piano with the strings struck by hammers. This is a modern reproduction.

42. An early fortepiano of six octaves built by John Broadwood & Son, *c.* 1817. The mahogany case has rosewood and brass inlays and the original ivory keys. It is similar to the one given to Beethoven by the City of London in 1816.

43.   A square piano built by John Broadwood in 1807. Mahogany Sheraton case with satinwood banding, on frame stand with brass castors. The keyboard of 5½ octaves, is of ebony and ivory.

44. A six octave cabinet piano built by John Broadwood & Son, *c.* 1840. The case is made of 'Spanish' mahogany and contrasting rosewood with a brass grill front and decorated top.

45. A seven octave grand piano, of short 'drawing-room' grand dimensions, built by John Broadwood *c.* 1870. The case is of rosewood.

46.   This reed organ, a domestic instrument, was named the 'Improved Seraphine' and was built by Joseph Kirkman & Thomas White *c.* 1805.

47. The console and front cabinet of the organ of Holy Trinity Church, **Kings-**way, London.

48. A Wurlizter Pipe Organ originally built for an American millionaire then shipped to England and installed at the Regal Cinema, Kingston-upon-Thames in 1931. Eventually acquired by the British Piano Museum in 1972, and used there in conjunction with the Wurlitzer Automatic Reproducing Roll Player.

49. The lute was
popular instrument for
companiment in the
teenth and seventeenth c
turies, but has an e
longer history. It was a
the first instrument
attract a large body
written music. This theo
lute was made by M
Unverdorben (1535-70

50. The colascioni, a t
of three-stringed lute, m
by Antonio Baraptulius
Naples, 1535.

51.   The cittern is of the guitar family, with a flat back and usually four pairs of
strings which were plucked. An eighteenth-century instrument by Longman &
Broderick of 96 Cheapside & 18 Haymarket, London.

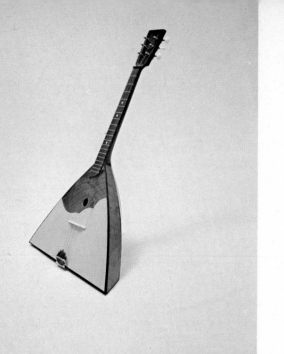

52 and 53. (*Top*) Th
balalaika, with its chara
teristic triangular body,
the Russian and Eas
European version of th
guitar with fretted finge
board. A modern versio
of this contrasts with
pandorina (*bottom*) of Ge
man origin made *c.* 168

54. The mandolin is a small instrument of the lute family common in Italy with regional varieties in Naples and Milan. It has a deep, pear-shaped body and fretted fingerboard.

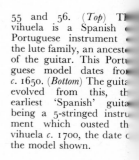

55 and 56. (*Top*) Th
vihuela is a Spanish
Portuguese instrument
the lute family, an ances
of the guitar. This Port
guese model dates fro
c. 1650. (*Bottom*) The guit
evolved from this, th
earliest 'Spanish' guita
being a 5-stringed instru
ment which ousted th
vihuela *c.* 1700, the date
the model shown.

57. The popularity of lute and guitar encouraged many mechanical and national variants such as this harp lute guitar.

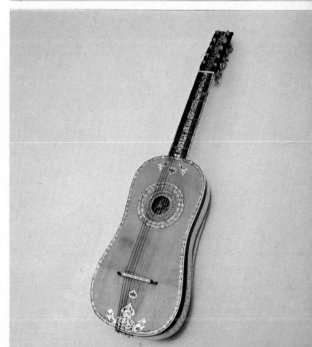

58. A German guitar made by Jacobus Stadler in 1624.

59.   The modern Spanish guitar, now made in all countries, returned to popularity with the enthusiasm for folk and popular music and jazz. It is a sturdy, resonant instrument, now often mass-produced.

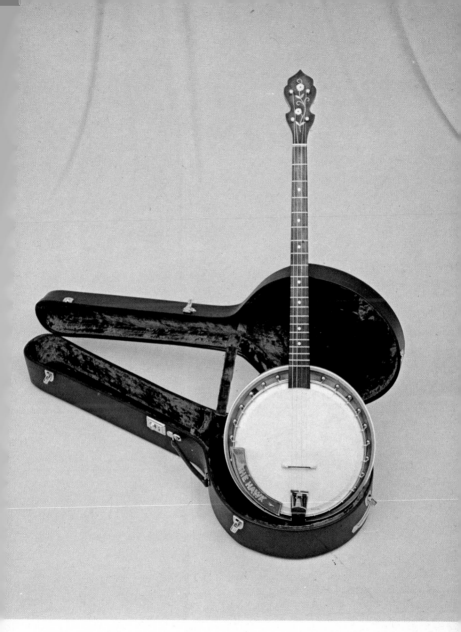

60. The banjo remained most common in America where it was developed from an African instrument brought over by the slaves. It also has many variants, big and small, varying numbers of strings, frets, etc.

61.   The cimbalom is the most common example of a percussive stringed instrument and is played with a pair of wooden beaters. It is generally found, as in this example, on legs, piano-style. Particularly popular in mid-European countries like Hungary.

62. Various stringed percussion from East and West including the psaltery (*middle left*); the qanum (*right*), pantaleon (*bottom*).

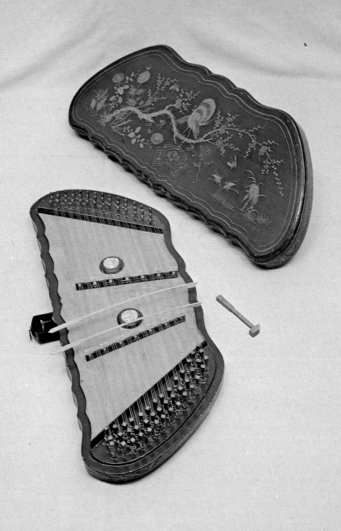

63. Another representative of the dulcimer or stringed percussion family is the Yang chin. This Far Eastern dulcimer has 14 sets of brass strings struck by two bamboo sticks.

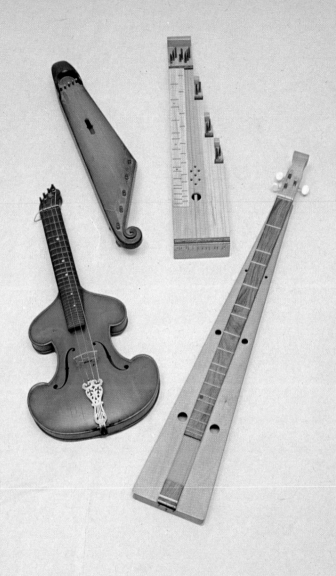

64. Many Eastern and Western variants of the lute family exist in all shapes and sizes. Here are several examples, with the curious lute viol on the left.

65. The qanun is essentially a Middle-East psaltery with 24 sets of gut strings, three to each note. The strings are plucked with plectrums.

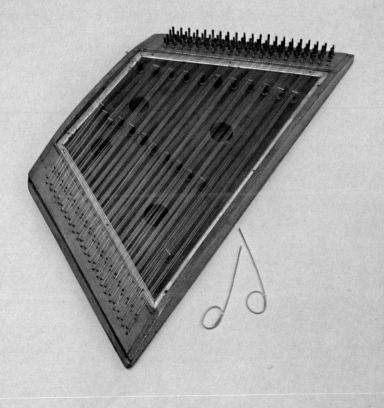

66. This is the best-known form of the dulcimer, with beaters. Compare this with the heavier cimbalom (61) which is generally mounted on legs.

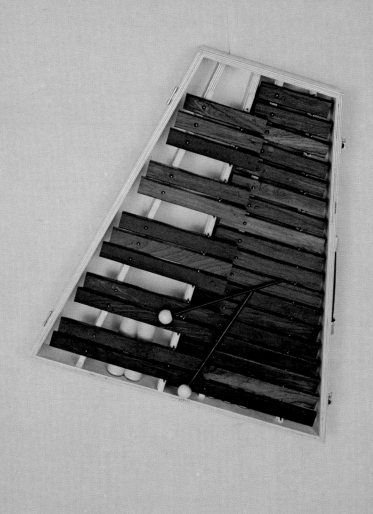

67. The xylophone has existed in many forms since ancient times. Basically it is a set of tuned wooden bars on a frame which allows them to be resonant. This is a portable instrument; usually it is on legs with tubular resonators under each bar.

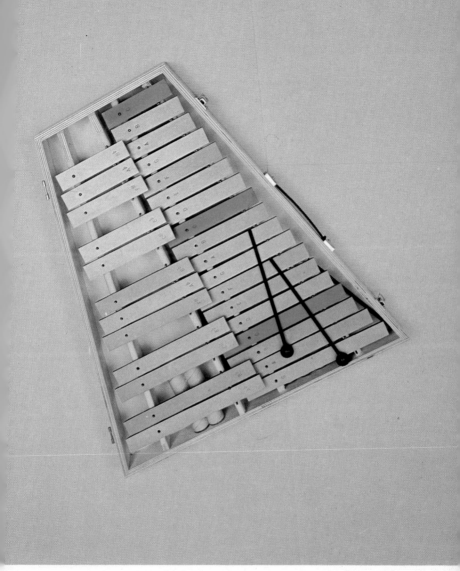

68. The glockenspiel is similar to the xylophone but with metal bars and is usually a table-top instrument as here. There is also a vertical marching version often in a lyre-like frame.

69. The kettle-drum obviously has a long ancestry through various primitive percussion instruments. A shallow kind is used by mounted cavalry. The deeper type, more generally known as timpani, have become sophisticated instruments and some have pedal tuning.

70. (*Top*) The sidedrum or tom-tom is a regular item of modern percussion. (*Bottom*) The snare-drum is one of the most distinctive types, with the wire snares stretched under the top skin producing the familiar rattling sound.

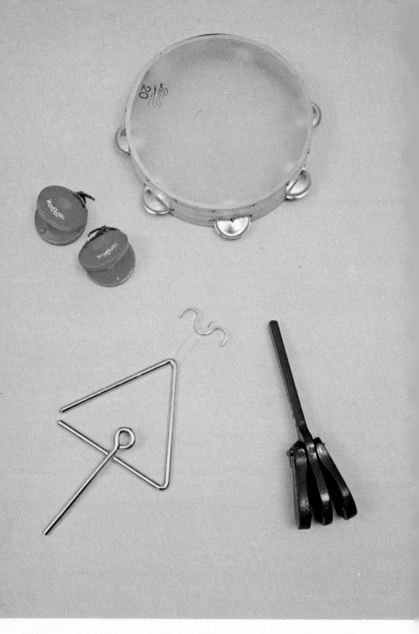

71. Among the multitude of effects used in the modern percussion section are items of great antiquity—the tinkling triangle (*bottom*), the clacking castanets (*left*), the rattling tambourine (*top*), and various items to produce clicks, bangs and shakes.

72.   The gong is very much connected with the Far East and most originated from there. In more recent times they have been manufactured in mid-Europe. The larger ones are capable of producing an incredible volume of sound.

73. Military drums are specialised versions of their orchestral counterparts
They were designed to be portable and were usually highly decorated for display.

74. The jazz percussion unit is designed for maximum operation by one man. Additions not usually found in orchestral percussion include foot pedals to operate the bass drum and cymbals, thus freeing the hands for more exhibitionist employment.

75. An essential part of the modern musical scene is the electrification and amplification of various instruments. The resulting sound lacks the purity of traditional instruments and too high a level of sound is a common fault, but it does allow for compacter instruments as the electrified guitar (*left*) and bass (*right*) show.

76. The hurdy gurdy (a name often misapplied to a portable feed organ) is a stringed instrument, with the strings stopped by keys. The sound, including a drone, is produced by a rotating wheel, hand-wound.

77. The barrel organ was a popular street instrument in the nineteenth century and still thrives on the Continent. The mechanism was operated by a rotating barrel set with pins. The instrument comes in various sizes, from portative to vast dance hall complexes.

78. The street piano usually worked on the same principal as the barrel organ, the pins setting the piano mechanism in action as it was turned.

79.   In pre-gramophone and radio days, numerous mechanical instruments were devised for home and salon use. The polyphon was operated by a large, mechanically driven disc with protrusions which activated the sound.

80. Musical boxes used some variation of the barrel or disc (both shown here) driven by clockwork motors to 'pluck' the tuned teeth. Each barrel or disc would be set with a number of tunes which slipped into action successively. Musical boxes came in all shapes and sizes and were invariably elegantly decorated and adorned.

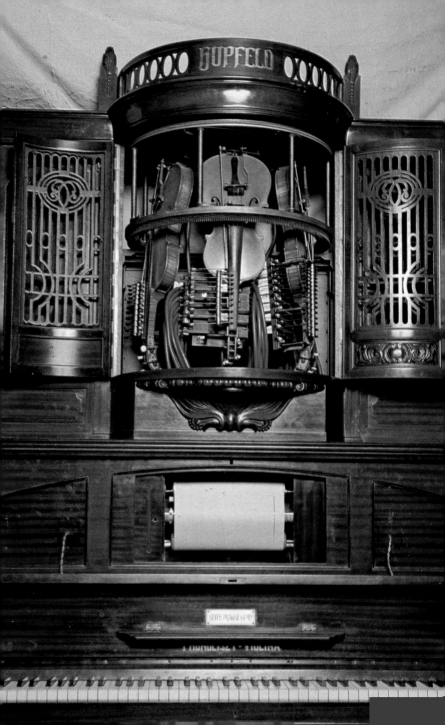

81. The mechanical contrivances got wilder and more wonderful. The roll-operated Hupfeld Phonolist Violina included three violins with continuous bow on the hurdy-gurdy principle and piano accompaniment. Coin-operated, it was made in 1909.

82. Gradually more and more mechanical instruments were operated from a single course of energy and folding books of punched cards replaced the barrel. In 'orchestrations' like this electrically driven model of 1899, whole orchestras were put into operation.

83. The East produces a multitude of colourful instruments. (*Right*) The Sarangi
and its bow, the Indian form of the fiddle. (*Centre*) The single-stringed ektara.

84. Various kinds of long-necked lute appear in most Eastern countries. The Indian version is the large-bodied sitar with seven metal strings, two of which are used as a drone.

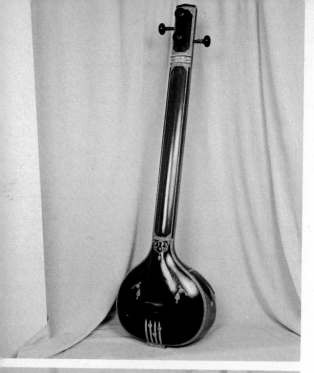

85. The tambura is similar to the sitar, but i without frets and only ha four strings. It is usec simply as a drone accom paniment to the other in struments.

86. The vina is the Indian form of the zither, traditionally a fanciful looking instrument with two large gourd resonators. A modernised version is coming into more common use.

37. The large drum is a mridangam and the smaller ones the well-known tabla.

88. All countries have their form of the pipes and drums. (*Below*) These Indian pipes are called shehnai and are seen with various flutes and a mountain horn.

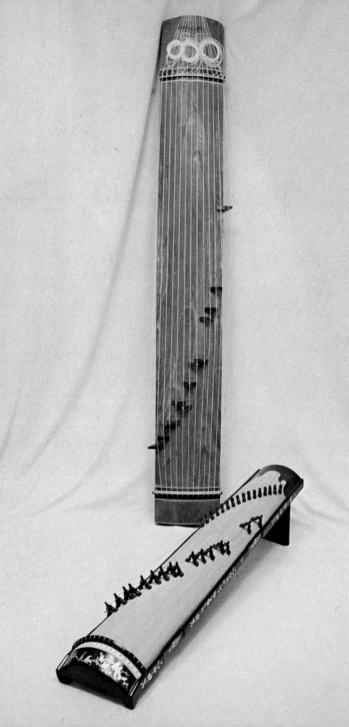

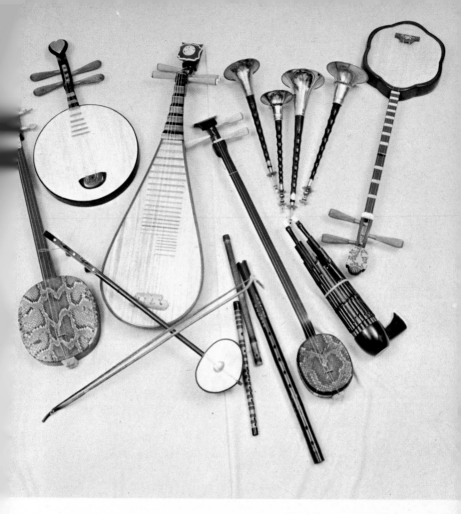

90. A group of Chinese instruments which includes (*clockwise from top left*) a gue-gin, a pi-pa, a group of Chinese shawms, a banjo, a shang or bamboo mouth organ, a reptile skin covered banjo, wau-xisos, a 2-stringed coconut violin and a larger skin covered banjo.

89. Two instruments from the Far East. At the back is the Japanese koto and in the front is the Cu-zheng, a Chinese instrument which, orchestrally, fills a similar niche.

91. Perhaps the gramophone is not everyone's idea of a musical instrument, but probably more people 'play' it today than any other. Cylinder machines like this Edison Bell model, *c.* 1900, were gradually superseded after Berliner's introduction of the flat disc machines.

7 The organ

The title of 'king of instruments' has ungrudgingly been given to the *organ*. In principle it reverts to the wind department, and one could say that the organ is simply a glorified bagpipe. In this case, in the simplest terms, the keyboard is used to operate a mechanism which puts into operation a varied range of pipes of both the penny-whistle and reed variety. In addition, it needs a constant supply of wind, supplied in the earlier instruments by hand-operated bellows, later by mechanical means. As more compact electronic instruments are developed, the organ has, to a limited extent, come back into the affluent home. But it is still a bit of an outsider among instruments, occasionally combining most effectively with the orchestra, but more generally a solo instrument whose size, complexity and expense keeps it rooted in churches and halls, unwritten for by many major composers; a producer of cumbersome sounds that many music-lovers find not particularly attractive.

The earlier organs had uncomplicated, woodwindy tones, which gave way, as the instrument's mechanics became more complex, to the massive and multifarious sounds of the bigger modern instruments. Those who do not like organs are probably deterred by their slightly 'un-natural' tones, that is timbres which don't quite sound like instruments blown by human beings, or the often overwhelming quantity and quality of sound or even the preponderance of dull and ponderous music that has been written for the instrument.

The organ, in some form or other, has probably been around for about two thousand years. The Greeks and Romans used quite sophisticated instruments. Then their development shifted to the Middle East and finally to Europe where crude and blatant sounding instruments seemed to have been to the general taste. Small 'portative' or portable organs were in common use in the thirteenth century, one hand operating a small keyboard with a row of flute pipes above, the other pumping a small set of bellows. By the mid-fourteenth century larger organs with three keyboards and pedals were in use. These achieved their effects by having several rows of pipes with valves allowing them to be put into operation simultaneously. In the fifteenth and sixteenth centuries 'stops' were added which operated on the pipes to make them sound an octave lower or higher as required and provided other intervals which could be sounded. With these additions the organ was rapidly becoming the instrument which could produce a massive orchestral sound in the hands of one player.

Reed pipes were now added to the *flute* or *flue* pipe and special pipes were developed which could approximately imitate various instrumental tones. The baroque organ of the seventeenth and eighteenth centuries was still, by modern standards, a very pure sounding instrument but with a limited range of expressiveness. The organ had, to some extent, the same problem as the other earlier keyboard instruments, the disadvantage of not being able to produce an expressive or graded tone. The subsequent developments were the addition of shutters which allowed the sound to be made louder or softer, the addition of stops to imitate as many orchestral instruments as possible and to produce a wide range of mixtures of these sounds.

It is putting it mildly to say that what we see of the organ *in situ* in church or hall is only the tip of the iceberg. The manuals and ranks of stops and artistically displayed rows of beautifully decorated pipes became as much a plaything of the architect as the organ-builder. It looks complicated enough, but behind the scenes lies a vast array of pumps, more pipes, and of course the involved mechanism needed to put all this into action. The mechanical or 'tracker' action had the one disadvantage of being rather noisy, but is generally preferred as it is more sensitive and achieves better phrasing and rhythm. However, a tracker action needs sufficient space to have the manuals and the works in one area. The frequent need to have the organ chamber well away from pipes led to the use of an electric action where the pressing of a key closes an electric circuit and the valves are opened by a remote motor. The remoteness of the player in some of the larger and more vulgar electric organs, such as were common in the cinemas of the 1930s, tended to make the organ sound very much a mechanical instrument. After the age of romantic excess and electronics, the tendency is to return to tracker action and well-balanced, purer tones. The splendid instrument in the Festival Hall in London is a modern example of an organ very nearly ideal in all respects.

The admirer of instruments for their shapes and sizes will undoubtedly get a maximum of enjoyment out of 'collecting' organs. Most of them are accessible to the viewer and there is tremendous satisfaction in simply seeing splendid church instruments, such as the 1893 Willis organ in Carshalton parish church or that noble monster in Eton College chapel. Even the few remaining examples of the vainglorious *cinema organ* have gathered a band of admirers. Indeed, one of the chief glories of Frank Holland's Piano Museum (see Appendix) is the Wurlitzer which came from the Regal Cinema in Kingston-upon-Thames where it had been installed in 1931. In its present home it has even the added sophistication of being coupled to the only Wurlitzer Automatic Reproducing Roll Player ever to have been installed in Europe, playing, without the touch of human hand, a repertoire of sixty rolls made by various organists. The final touch to this impressive installation is the coupling of a Steinway grand, which can be operated both mechanically and manually from the organ manual. For all those organ enthusiasts who demand a specification of instruments heard and recorded and, as a tribute to man's ingenuity, the specification of the 'Regal' Wurlitzer is as follows:

SPECIFICATION OF THE WURLITZER ORGAN

PEDAL

Tuba Profunda	16
Diaphone	16
Bourdon	16
English Horn	8
French Trumpets	8
Diaphonic Diapason	8
Tibia Clausa	8
Saxophone	8
Cello	8

Flute 8
Piano 16
Bass Drum   Bass Drum Roll
Kettle Drum   Crash Cymbal   Cymbal
(The above five on first touch, with switch to second touch)
Accompaniment to Pedal
Great to Pedal
Three adjustable toe pistons

ACCOMPANIMENT
Second Touch
English Horn	8
French Trumpet	8
Great Octave to Accompaniment	
Tibia Clausa	8
Saxophone	8
Kinura	8
Piccolo	4
Xylophone (Tap)	37 notes
Triangle	
Tambourine Slap	

(Great Octave to Accompaniment coupler
replaced Violin 8)

GREAT
English Horn	T.C. 16
Tuba Profunda	16
Diaphone	16
Tibia Clausa	T.C. 16
Saxophone	T.C. 16
Contra Viole	T.C. 16
Bourdon	16
Vox Humana	T.C. 16
English Horn	8
Harmonica Tuba	8
French Trumpet	8
Open Diapason	8
Tibia Clausa	8
Saxophone	8
Kinura	8
Violin	8
Violin Celeste	8
Krumet	8
Concert Flute	8
Vox Humana	8
Harmonic Clarion	4
Octave	4
Piccolo	4
Saxophone	4
Violin	4
Octave Celeste	4
Flute	4
Twelfth (Tibia)	2⅔
Twelfth	2⅔
Piccolo (Tibia)	2
Piccolo	2
Tierce	1⅗
Piano	16
Piano	8
Piano	4
Cathedral Chimes	25 notes
Xylophone (Tap)	37 notes
Xylophone (Re-it)	37 notes
Glockenspiel	30 notes
Orchestra Bells	30 notes
Chrysoglott	49 notes
Snare Drum	Tambourine
Castanets	Chinese Block
Tom Tom	Solo Sub to Great
Sub Octave	Unison Off
Octave	Eight adjustable thumb pistons

GREAT
Second Touch
Saxophone	T.C. 16
English Horn	8
Tibia Clausa	8
Saxophone	8

ACCOMPANIMENT
Contra Viole	T.C. 16
Vox Humana	T.C. 16
Saxophone	T.C. 16
English Horn	8
Harmonic Tuba	8
French Trumpet	8
Open Diapason	8
Tibia Clausa	8
Saxophone	8
Kinura	8
Violin	8
Violin Celeste	8
Concert Flute	8
Vox Humana	8
Octave	4
Piccolo	4
Saxophone	4
Violin	4
Octave Celeste	4
Flute	4
Vox Humana	4
Twelfth	2⅔
Piccolo	2
Piano	16
Piano	8
Piano	4
Mandolin	
Xylophone (Tap)	37 notes
Chrysoglott	49 notes
Snare Drum	Tambourine
Castanets	Chinese Block
Tom Tom	Solo to Accompaniment
	Eight adjustable thumb pistons

SOLO
Tuba Profunda	16
Diaphone	16
Tibia Clausa	T.C. 16
Saxophone	T.C. 16
English Horn	8
Harmonic Tuba	8
French Trumpet	8
Open Diapason	8
Tibia Clausa	8
Saxophone	8
Kinura	8
Krumet	8
Violin	8
Harmonic Clarion	4
Octave	4
Piccolo	4
Saxophone	4
Cathedral Chimes	25 notes
Xylophone (Re-it)	37 notes
Glockenspiel	30 notes
Orchestra Bells	30 notes
Chrysoglott	49 notes
Five adjustable thumb pistons	

TREMULANTS
Main	Solo	Tuba
English Horn/Saxophone	Vox Humana	

SWELL PEDALS
Main	Sole
Piano/Main Solo coupler	
General Crescendo	

ACCESSORIES

Two sforzando pedals
Vibraphone (on Chrysoglott)
Chrysoglott damper

EFFECTS

By push buttons:
Auto Horn   Door Bell

Steamboat Whistle

By stopkeys on key rail:
Horse Hooves   Surf   Bird Whistle
Fire Gong (Re-it)   Siren

By toe pistons:
Surf   Fire Gong   Triangle
Horse Hooves   Bird Whistle

VIEW OF THE COMPLEX PIPE ARRANGEMENT IN A MODERN ORGAN

133

8

Fretted instruments

After the organ's display of musical might it is pleasant to turn to some quieter instruments – to an important group of stringed instruments which, while they have not had the orchestral importance of the *violin* family, have become variously established as solo instruments. These are the 'fretted' instruments which have the common characteristic of a number of strings that are plucked and a fingerboard into which small bars or 'frets' are inserted at intervals of a semitone. These are essential in that, while the violin is more often than not playing a single melodic note which can fairly easily be located on the fingerboard, the fretted instruments are frequently called upon to play chords using all the strings and it would be almost impossible to finger accurately four or more strings simultaneously.

The honourable forefather of most of the modern fretted instruments is the *lute* which came to Europe from the Middle East in the thirteenth century. The early instrument had four strings which were struck with a quill or plectrum. These, as in many instruments of this kind, became pairs of strings. By the fifteenth century the lute more often had six pairs of strings or 'courses' and was more frequently played with the fingers, and by this time had already become more or less perfected. It was a delicate instrument, its large pear-shaped body made of very thin wood, generally pine. It had a broad neck with a characteristic backward slanting peg-box and the frets were simply pieces of thick gut tied round the neck at intervals and correctly spaced by the player. It became an enormously popular instrument both for domestic use and in the hands of virtuoso players, reigning for some four centuries, as the piano was to do in the nineteenth and twentieth centuries, as the chief domestic instrument. As a result some magnificent music was written for the instrument by the great lutenists. In 1603, for instance, Besard's *Thesaurus Harmonicus* collected together over four hundred pieces by composers from all over Europe. Later, much of its music was taken over by the guitar, but in recent times the lute has been revived to play its own repertoire with matchless delicacy, including many fine songs with lute accompaniment by the great Elizabethan composers.

There were other instruments in the lute family which did not attain such great popularity. The *theorbo* was a larger lute with longer strings and even longer bass strings accommodated on a second peg-box. It generally had single strings, the group of extra long bass strings being tuned to chords and not stopped by the fingers, while the rest were used as in the lute. The attempts to build up a consort of fretted instruments led to even deeper bass instruments to give a solid foundation to the group, including the *Roman theorbo* or *chitarrone* extending to about 1·5 m (5 ft) in length to accommodate some long bass strings.

The lute itself was adapted to various shapes and sizes including a double-strung lute, working on the same principle as the theorbo and often known as the *theorbo-lute*. It had considerable popularity in France. Constant adaptations and strengthening of the original instruments made a pure-bred early lute a great rarity and their extreme fragility did not help. Nowadays one is most likely to hear a modern copy to cater for the modern interest in its music promoted by the Dolmetsch family.

The *guitar*, eventually to become even more popular than the lute, was not actually a descendant but grew up alongside it. The lute dominated them because of its delicate and expressive tones. The guitar's true ancestor, the *cittern* was a popular instrument because of its comparative simplicity. It was tuned somewhat like the modern *ukulele* with four or five sets of double wire strings or courses which gave it a bright tone. It was popular as an instrument to accompany voices and much used as the barber's shop instrument of its day. It had a round body, shallow and flat backed and could easily be hung

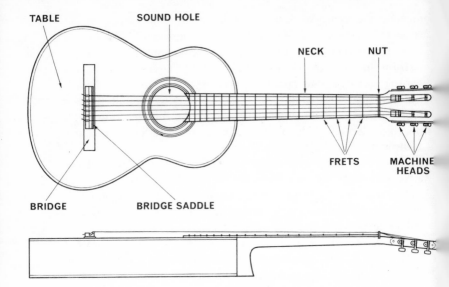

SHAPE OF A MODERN GUITAR

on a wall. Similar in nature, but varied in shape, were the *orpharion*, the *pandora* or *bandora* and, nearest to the modern guitar, the *gittern*. A gittern of around 1330 is preserved in Warwick Castle. Some of these instruments had gut strings, some wire. Music for the *cittern* was being written as late as the mid-seventeenth century. All these instruments then gave way to the guitar, the English model looking somewhat like a lute with a pear-shaped body, flat at the back rather than rounded like the lute's, and with the same backward slanting peg-box.

The early *Spanish guitar* or *vihuela* (there was also a bowed version) began to flourish in the sixteenth century, declined in the seventeenth and began to flourish again in the eighteenth century as it caught the fancy of many European composers. In Spain, it was always popular as a solo instrument and its rhythms are copied in orchestral terms in what we think of as typical Spanish music. By the end of the eighteenth century the guitar was established as a six-string instrument

136

with metal frets which was perfected by many makers outside Spain; made of exotic woods like bird's eye maple, walnut and rosewood intermingled with pine. It is a robust instrument, its large body producing the necessary volume even with fairly thick wood. A race of dedicated virtuosi, ranging from Sor to Segovia, established it in the concert-hall and many of the great composers wrote occasional pieces for it, but its music flourished in the hands of lesser composers who specialised in the instrument right up to the present day. It became popular in Austrian folk and light music, spread to Latin America and thence to North America. Its great popularity today was due first to the advocacy of the virtuoso Segovia and secondly to the instrument's endless adaptability to folk-based popular music.

In Italy the lute-like *mandolin* had its own success, deriving from a small lute known as a *mandora* and a wire-strung plectrum cittern called the *chitarra battente*. Small, high-pitched with a very distinct tone colour, an inimitable style of tremolo playing was used in Neapolitan popular music and still survives.

The guitar certainly dominated. But in Spain and Portugal, and especially in the South American countries, various instruments were devised to form string bands of wide ranging pitch and timbre. These near relatives include the *guitarillo*, the *requinte* and *tenore*, all smaller-scaled guitars; the deeper *laud* and *bandurria* and the Portuguese *guitarra*, still somewhat like the English model, made to accompany the guitar, which, in Portugal is called the *violão*.

In Russia similar instruments developed. A whole family of triangular-bodied, three-stringed *balalaikas*, a *domra* which resembles a cittern and the extremely complicated multi-stringed *bandoura*. In North America, the guitar developed into a twelve-string giant, alongside an African-bred instrument called the *banjo* which differed from all the other fretted instruments by having a body which, in essence, is like a *tambourine*, with a vellum body stretched over a wooden hoop.

Starting as an instrument which could be made by the poorer Negro musicians, the banjo developed into a manufactured instrument with an added metal resonator on its back. Standard instruments are the five-string finger style banjo, with its extra high string tuned part way along the neck, used as a melody instrument, and the four-string plectrum banjo used as an accompanying instrument. The more elaborate *zither-banjo* followed for virtuoso use, and for the amateur who liked to double on other instruments there was the *tenor-banjo* tuned in fifths for the violinist, the *banjo-mandolin* and the single string *banjoline*. The banjo, with its percussive, twangy tone, was very popular in early jazz and minstrel shows and became very much a craze in the 1920s. Later it was supplanted in popular music by the plectrum played guitar. For popular and less-skilled use there was the *ukulele*, basically a very small guitar, simple to strum, tune and play, and the small *ukulele-banjo* or *banjulele* (as popularised by George Formby) with similar tuning.

The *Hawaiian guitar*, originally a fretted instrument, gave up its frets to be held flat on the knees. The strings are stopped by a sliding metal bar, which makes it capable of intriguing glissando effects.

The Austrian *zither* is a cross between the harp (developing from the psaltery) and the guitar (in technique and intent). In appearance it is a flat box (there is no neck) across which are stretched two sets of strings. One is a set of melody strings with frets which are fingered by the left hand and struck with a plectrum worn on the thumb of the right hand while the other fingers pluck a number of strings which are tuned into ready-made harmonies. It is an extremely complicated instrument to play but its effect is delightful and unique.

The zither leads to another vast family of hybrids which have tuned strings like a harp but, at the same time, have hankerings toward being keyboard instruments, albeit without keyboards, because their strings are hit with small beaters. The two best-known members of this family are the *dulcimer*, an instrument often heard in biblical times, and the mid-European *cimbalom*. The latter has an open, box-like body on legs and a damper pedal. It is played with tremendous dexterity and a very effective tremolo by Hungarian virtuosi and their emulators elsewhere. There is a staggering number of these horizontal multi-string instruments, with fantastically varied hollow bodies, their strings plucked, stroked or hit with beaters or mallets. Indeed, nearly every country in the world has its own particular variety. The English virtuoso, John Leech, in his concerts often demonstrates the *cimbalom*, *psaltery*, the Middle Eastern *qanun* and *santur*, the Eastern *cheng koto* and *yang chin*, and various dulcimers from the Appalachians to Ireland.

It is not, however, only tuned strings that are struck with small hammers. There is a whole range of bars of stone (going back to prehistoric times), wood or metal which, if laid on felt or some material that allows them to resonate across two strips of wood, can be tuned to the chromatic scale and hit with hard or soft hammers to produce some pleasing and percussive tones. This technique is commonly applied to the *xylophone* (which generally has wooden bars), the *glockenspiel* (metal bars), which also has an upright model, the *lyra-glockenspiel*, for marching bands, the *marimba* (a deep-toned xylophone played with soft hammers) and the modern *vibraphone*. The xylophone's resonances are improved in present-day models by having metal tubes fixed below the bars. In the vibraphone there is a small, electrically-driven fan rotating on an axle inside the tubes, which produces a continuous vibrato and a sound very familiar in modern jazz circles. Another tuned instrument, used in the orchestra for romantic 'bells across the meadow' type of effects, is the tubular bells, or chimes, simply a tuned set of metal tubes hung vertically in a frame and hit with a raw-hide hammer.

9

Percussion instruments

In considering rival claims of antiquity among instruments, the percussion, as already suggested, must surely have come first. The family tree goes so far back and is so full of offspring, that it would be impossible to pinpoint the true beginnings. Percussion always has been, and still is, basic to the life of primitive tribes, serving practical purposes, like sending messages, as well as being used for ritual and entertainment. The gourd or hollowed log probably came first but the idea of stretching a skin over a hooped shape also goes back into antiquity.

The most important items of orchestral percussion today are certainly the *timpani*, of most interest and effect because they can be tuned and thus, to a limited extent, are also melodic instruments. Known in early times as *kettledrums*, there are two basic sizes, a small, shallow marching drum which is first mentioned around the twelfth century and which came into Europe about the time of the Crusades under the name of *nakers;* and the larger and deeper kind which would be slung over the backs of horses and other creatures. Illustrations of these go back to about AD 600. Of Islamic origin, they were always used in pairs, tuned to two different notes fundamental to the key being used. In many African cultures they are used in larger numbers in drum ensembles. Kettledrums were used in English cavalry regiments from the sixteenth century where they provided the accompaniment to trumpets, and are still in particular favour with the royal household cavalry regiments. The original orchestral instruments were these same military instruments and their limited tuning capacities restricted their use. Composers from Haydn onwards found the timpani essential to their musical ideas and timpani were rapidly developed into the large, mellow-sounding instrument that we know today, starting with a basic pair, one slightly larger than the other, to provide the fundamental harmonies. The problem for the timpanist has always been to get his instruments retuned for changes of key and the composer had to be careful to allow time for this delicate operation. The mechanics of doing this were steadily improved as the quality of the instruments was generally advanced, which was fortunate, as a composer like Beethoven made considerable demands on his timpani. By 1830 Berlioz was needing two pairs of timpani and two timpanists. It is easy to understand the difficulty of the player's task when one realises that he generally has to tune his instruments ready for the coming key change while the orchestra is still playing in the key to which he is already tuned. Although the approximate number of turns to the tuning handle becomes a matter of habit, the finer tuning must still be done by ear as temperature and humidity have a quite considerable effect on the tension of the drum's heads. Nowadays there is a general move from vellum or goat-skin heads to plastic ones which are less affected, but the timpanist will always have a spare head to hand in case of breakage. The last development in timpani was the use of variable tuning by means of a foot-pedal which has given the instrument its final flexibility, allowing for written solo passages and the use of glissandi. A variety of drum sticks are used, varying from soft to hard and occasionally the instruments are muted by putting a piece of soft cloth on the head.

The timpani occupy one player full-time in the orchestra while one or more percussionist handles the rest of the instruments which, for best effect, are used far more sparingly. These include the *side drum* which is descended from the early *tabor* and is more generally known as the *snare drum* as it has a number of gut or wire strings stretched across its lower head which vibrate against it with a rattling sound when the upper head is struck. The snares can be released, allowing the drum to be quickly muted. Occasionally it is even played without the snares in operation. Again, the nature of the snare-drum is essentially military and its rolls, drags, flams and paraddiddles (some of the basic beats) are familiar from their use in military band music.

The *tenor drum*, a larger instrument without snares, is generally played with soft sticks. It is not used a great deal orchestrally, but is common in military and pipe bands. The *bass drum* is popular in the orchestra for its occasional rich effect. The orchestral instrument has generally only one head, which gives less sustained vibration, but the marching instrument will usually be double-sided.

The *tambourine* is, in effect, a small one-sided drum with a vellum stretched over a circular band of wood into which are inset at intervals small pairs of miniature cymbals or jingles. Such an instrument can be seen in a Roman relief, known as 'The Triumph of Bacchus', which dates back to the second century AD. A useful adjunct to dancer, carried and shaken in one hand, struck with the fingers of the other hand, it produces an effective orchestral roll if a moistened thumb is drawn across the head.

The *cymbals* go back to the earliest civilisations. Small, delicate-sounding tuned cymbals known as *crotales* were found in ancient Egypt, Greece and Rome. The clashing cymbals were used in ancient Greek rites, accompanied by the beat of the *tympanum*, to excite the worshippers and their larger modern counterparts perform a similar role in the Albert Hall. Pairs of cymbals, one in each hand, can offer an impressive crash or a sustained shimmer of sound. A single cymbal can be struck with drumsticks, stroked with a brush, or even played with a bow on its edge. In the dance band the cymbal becomes even more a rhythm instrument with a pair mounted on a stand one above the other so that they can be continuously operated with a foot pedal.

The simplest of all instruments is possibly the *triangle*, a single piece of metal bent into a triangular shape with the two ends left just apart. Suspended on a strap or string so that it is free to vibrate, it is struck on its outside edge by a piece of metal to produce a delicate but penetrating sound, or in rapid succession on its inner edges to produce a prolonged tinkle.

The percussionist is called upon to produce a multitude of effects on a wide variety of additional instruments – *clappers* and *rattles*, *castanets*, *bells* of all kinds, various gourds and boxes and, most impressive of all, the *gong*, the deep-rimmed kind producing a note of definite pitch, the shallow flat gong or *tam-tam* a note of indefinite pitch. A quite shattering sound can be produced from a roll with a soft-headed stick, and it is quite understandable why the gong should be so often linked with the religious ceremonies of the East where it originated.

The craftsmanship that goes into the making of percussion instruments has a real blend of science and intuitive art, producing shapes that are both functional and graceful, scientific shapes that have grown from natural ones. The practical use to which instruments are put is nowhere better illustrated than in the subtle variations in percussion instruments within different fields of music. The rambling and often fairly drab assortment of pieces that spreads itself across the back of a symphony orchestra and is operated by several men is very different from the compact one-man-band outfit, flashily decorative, that is to be found in the jazz or dance band. Here the object is to have as many items as possible within reach so that the hands can switch from one to the other instantaneously while the feet are busily operating pedals for the *high hat cymbals* or *bass drum*. The designs for these instruments, which developed in the 1920s and 30s, are of the art-nouveau style of cinemas and cinema organs of that period, jazzy and crude, impressive through the sheer weight of vulgarity. The military band instruments, however, are a delight in all ways. Practical in that they have to be carried and stand up to a partly outdoor life, they are decorated with lavish richness coupled with dignity. The drums bear the badges and battle honours and the brass instruments are often splendidly engraved. It is a paradox that the needs of war and the disciplines of uniform have produced such a rich addition to musical life.

10 *Mechanical instruments*

So far the instruments discussed have been those built to be played expertly and lovingly; instruments whose shapes and characters have had a delicate evolution, staying as close to nature as possible. Mechanical sophistication has been contrived to aid fingers and lips to get the best possible sound with the maximum of ease, but they ask for dedication and skill to achieve their best effects.

But not everybody can be a Heifetz or a Horowitz, a Benny Goodman or an Earl Hines. The love of music is universal; it is a human need. Today the non-player and the inexpert have only to turn a knob or two and they have the world's music at their finger-tips. In the days before the gramophone and radio, there was an equal hunger for music, partly satisfied by a more widespread cult of amateur music-making which resulted in vast sales of sheet music and parlour pianos and other instruments. But bad playing is often worse than none at all, so there was always a demand either for instruments which simplified the needed techniques and, as man's ingenuity advanced, instruments which required no human skills at all. Such instruments have their own brand of graciousness and good design to offer but, quite often, move into an area of grotesque improbability, with the charm of all things quaint and eccentric. A tour around a collection of mechanical and semi-mechanical instruments leaves an impression of a temporary visit to the imagined world of Lewis Carroll.

Before looking at the delightfully crackpot world of true mechanical instruments, one or two 'simplified' instruments must be mentioned. As long as the use of fingers is needed some skill will always be required, but several instruments were invented that at least gave some encouragement to the amateur manipulator. Such an instrument was the *hurdy-gurdy*. Its name not only became a universal one, applied to hand-wound instruments in the same way that we call all vacuum-cleaners 'hoovers' and all ball point pens 'biros', but was also applied quite erroneously to all kinds of *barrel organs* and *street pianos*. This probably arises from the fact that the hurdy-gurdy was commonly used in the mid-eighteenth century by street musicians who then changed to the portable street organ or piano as these became available. The hurdy-gurdy had ancient origins but was first commercially made in the early eighteenth century as a musical toy for the upper classes. It then went down the social scale to end up again as a folk instrument, a role to which its bagpipe-like tones were, in fact, better suited.

Most hurdy-gurdies were made in France, where it is called the *vielle*, and some of the early ones were simply guitars or lutes with mechanism added. The hurdy-gurdy is basically a stringed instrument, generally resembling the old *viola d'amore* in shape, in which the strings are actuated by the resined rim of a wooden wheel which is rotated by a handle at the rear of the instrument. Two, three or four of its strings provide a drone bass, being tuned generally to the chord of C or G (these are called *bourdons*), while one or two strings called *chanterelles* are used for the melody, their notes obtained by the strings being stopped by keys or tangents that press against them from the side. Skill is certainly needed to produce a pleasant sound, but even so its end result is fairly weird and discordant, and there is no orchestral use for such an instrument. An instrument of this nature goes back to Roman times when it was called an *organistrum*. The sliding rods or tangents were developed in the thirteenth century and the instruments became quite elaborate and highly decorated. There are some marvellous examples in the Victoria and Albert Museum.

Simplified harps with ready-made chords have already been mentioned. The disadvantage of all stringed instruments, from a strictly amateur point of view, is that they still have to be tuned, an operation that tends to be more rather than less complicated as tuning needs a good ear and considerable skill. There must have been a great number of lyre-harps and similar contraptions lying untuned and unloved in Victorian attics. Even such basic instruments as ukuleles and banjos tend to get neglected for the same reason. In 1870 the well-known firm of Distin put on the market a *ballad horn* intended 'for amateurs to enable them to play off the top line from pianoforte music or songs without transposition. It is exceedingly easy to blow and has an exquisitely mellow tone.' That took some believing and the ballad horn went noiselessly into extinction – one had first to learn to blow correctly!

In fact what was really needed for the dedicated amateur was an instrument which, after being pumped or wound up, did all the rest. Such instruments have always been produced and met with a fair success. The most widespread principle of operation, allowing notes to be played in a fixed and fairly complex order, was that of the barrel: a wooden or metal cylinder with pins set in it. As the cylinder rotates the pins operate in the required order, singly or several at a time, whatever is going to produce the ultimate sound. The principle was probably used first to operate a series of hammers to strike bells; something of the sort had been used in musical clocks dating back to the seventeenth century. The next idea was to have a series of metal strips, like a comb with teeth of increasing length. This is the basis of the *musical box* which started its years of popularity in the first quarter of the nineteenth century. Progressing from hand-wound instruments to refined clockwork mechanisms and adding additional effects like a set of miniature bells, drums and other percussive toys, the musical box was immensely popular by the middle of the century. The mechanism usually came in beautifully decorated boxes and offered a varied repertoire because it had multiple sets of pins brought into operation by the cylinder moving into a new position as each tune was completed. A similar principle was used in the *polyphons* which had a flat disc with pins instead of a cylinder. It was simple to replace a disc, rather like putting on another record. Some of the instruments had delightfully rich tones and the forerunner of the modern juke-box was to be found in coin-operated instruments that were mainly manufactured in Germany.

The same principle could be applied to a small organ, the pins opening and shutting a battery of pipes. The hand-turned or mechanical mechanism also operated a set of bellows to supply the wind. Starting as the small *portable organ*, still frequently seen in the 1920s in the hands of the travelling Italian organ grinder with his inevitable monkey, the *barrel organ* was developed into some mighty instruments that are still quite a common sight, particularly in Holland where the street organ is very popular. Inevitably the barrel, which was by now too big to be easily changed but could only offer a limited repertoire, had to be replaced by something more flexible. The revolution came with the invention, in the 1890s, of the book organ by the celebrated maker Anselmo Gavioli.

The mechanism of the mechanical organ now became like that of the real organ: each pipe was operated by a small set of bellows which, with a constant supply of air, was operated by a series of linked punched cards passing through the machine over a kind of mouth-organ. As the holes in the paper passed over the corresponding hole the air was allowed through to the appropriate bellow and even allowed a variation in the duration of the note by having longer and shorter holes. Once there was such an easy way of feeding information to pipes, the bellows could be made to operate any additional instruments. Some of the big dance-hall organs became miniature orchestras with wind, percussion and even stringed instruments put into operation to build up on the basic pipes. The *fairground organs*, with their equally romantic steam engines providing the necessary power, hold an undiminished attraction and, thank goodness, many surviving ones are being preserved by dedicated enthusiasts.

A parallel development was applied to the piano family. The once common *street piano* (often wrongly called a barrel organ or even a hurdy-gurdy) was again first operated by the pinned barrel, hand-turned, operating the normal piano action just as the fingers might have done. These 'pianos' were mainly made in Italy or Spain and, once again, their delightfully decorative appearance has meant that many of the surviving examples are being saved from the scrap-heap.

The introduction of the perforated book also made it possible to feed an unlimited repertoire to the piano, which had to incorporate hand- or foot-operated bellows to make use of this new system. As applied to the domestic piano, a long and replaceable roll of thin paper could be used and in the late-nineteenth century there was a tremendous demand for *piano-players* and *pianolas* from those who found a little physical exercise more rewarding than years of practising the piano.

Two systems were largely employed. The first was embodied in the *pianola*, where the whole mechanism was in a separate cabinet that could be moved up to any piano and from which felted hammers protruded over the piano keys, playing them as if they were mechanical fingers. The mechanism generally extended over a range of 65 notes. Many enthusiasts swear by the accuracy and subtlety of this early 65-note system. The *pianola* was superseded by the *player-piano*, although the previous trade name lingered to be used indiscriminately. The mechanism of the player-piano was incorporated into the body of the piano in permanent form, and instead of hammers playing on the keys, the bellows operated the piano action directly, cutting out at least one intermediate movement and giving a more silent and instant operation. The whole normal 88-note range of the piano was used and the instrument could also be used as a normal piano.

Fairly primitive systems were then electrically operated and were often installed in amusement arcades where they became known as *nickleodeons*, especially in America. Certain makers like Duo-Art, Welte Mignon and Ampico perfected the electrically-operated grand piano-player into an instrument of great sensitivity. An instrument in good order could reproduce the playing of the pianist who originally cut the roll with a great degree of accuracy, repeating every nuance of timing and dynamics. The piano-player thus becomes a fascinating source of historical documentation bringing back the art of virtuosi, classical and jazz, who made their reputations long before the gramophone record could give a decent duplication of a performance. It is quite uncanny to listen to one of these instruments playing itself. It was easy, on the other hand, to fake performances, and many makers could not resist punching a few extra holes in the roll to produce performances that would be beyond the powers of anyone with the usual equipment of ten fingers.

The ingenuity of some of the mechanical pianos put into public-houses in the late nineteenth century is almost beyond belief. There were instruments, penny-operated, that added percussion, xylophone and mandolin effects, and even saxophone reeds. Automatic roll changing was incorporated and, in America, there was even an instrument that actuated a set of model racehorses so that the customers could have bets on which would be first past the winning post while they listened to their music.

One of the most delightful of them all, to my mind, is the *Hupfeld Phonolist Violina* which can be seen and heard in the famous Piano Museum. Three violins, operated by a rotating cylinder bow on the old hurdy-gurdy principle, their strings stopped by ghostly mechanical fingers, make a delightful string trio accompanied by player-piano that offers a splendidly authentic recreation of the sounds to be heard in an Edwardian tea-room. The instrument was built in 1909.

Graced by a variety of musically suggestive patent names the variety of mechanical instruments is endless. They all suffered a mortal blow at the coming of the gramophone and radio and now mainly languish, with loving care bestowed, in various museums. Now, of course, even the early *gramophone*, with its cylinders and massive discs, handles and horns, is a museum piece with a history going back some hundred years – but that is another story.

This brief historical voyage of discovery has been mainly among instruments of European origin, but if we are thinking of instruments from an aesthetic point of view it would be a pity not to make passing mention of instruments from other continents. Many of our own instruments originated in the Middle and Far East or Africa. The charm and attraction of Indian, Arabic, Chinese and African instruments is that they have remained, in appearance at least, far more primitive and true objects of craftsmanship. They look hand-made and full of the natural curves that have been lost in some stereotyped factory-made instruments.

Their mechanics will not have the same impact on us because they work within different idioms, using scales which sound strange to our ears. Fundamentally it is a matter of the octave (which is common to all musics) being split into a different, sometimes more numerous, number of degrees. The complexity of some Indian instruments, for example, seems overwhelming. The commonest instrument is the *vina*, usually with seven strings and 24 metal frets on its long keyboard and two curious balloon-like sound chambers at either end. The *setar* or *sitar* is equally popular in northern India. It has movable frets and a louder and less refined tone than the *vina*. The *surbahar* is a huge instrument, a more involved version of the *sitar*. The *sarangi*, the Indian equivalent of the double-bass, has three thick strings, and is used mainly to accompany dancing; while the *tambura* is a four-stringed instrument used rather like an accompanying guitar. The Indian dulcimer or *quanum* is mainly found in the Punjab. Their flute is called a *vamsa* and their equivalent of the oboe is called the *surnai* in north India and *nagasaram* in the south. The common Indian horn is the *sringa*. The commonest drum is the *tabla*, with an infinite variety of regional instruments. Like all things Indian, they are colourfully painted and lovingly maintained.

Whether we turn to the Middle or Far East or to Africa, what we find, basically, is a set of drums, stringed, woodwind and brass instruments and tuned percussion, which corresponds roughly with what we have already found in Europe. To go into all the names in this short survey would invite confusion, but many are listed in the appended glossary of instruments, while the colour plates give a glimpse of their fascinating variety.

Even such a selective survey of instruments as this cannot help but give the feeling that understanding an instrument's mechanics teaches quite as much about the nature and appeal of music as simply listening to it as an abstract art. That music is deeply embedded in man's nature and essential to his full experience of life, is confirmed by the immense variety of instruments that there are in the world. The primitive tribesman cutting his reed pipe in the remaining jungles of the world is motivated by the same enthusiasm as the builder of a cathedral organ. His toil will eventually be rewarded by a mystical sense of pleasure, a sort of magic that lies in vibrating air and resonant materials; it is a subject at which we shall always nibble, but never wholly explain.

A concise glossary
of musical instruments

(those actually mentioned in the main text are indexed)

Accordion (*accordéon*, Fr; *fisarmonica*, Ital; *Handharmonika, Ziehhar-monika*, Ger.) Portable instrument with bellows that force air through metal reeds. Melody notes obtained by buttons or piano type keyboard (*piano-accordion*) for right hand; chords by buttons for left hand. 35

Aeolian harp Small twelve-string instrument, loosely strung so that it is set in motion by a current of air.

Aeoline Name patented in 1821–2 for a type of *harmonica*.

Aeoliphone Another name for the *wind-machine*.

Aelodion Keyed wind instrument similar to the *harmonium*, the sound produced from steel springs. Similar patented variations were the aelomelodicon, aeolopantalon and aeolsklavier.

Aerophor Air-pumping device that can be attached to a wind instrument to produce an indefinitely sustained note.

Ala bohemica A cross between a *zither* and *lute*, precursor of the Russian *bandoura*.

Albogon A Spanish *shawm* dating from the fourteenth century. Also known as *albogue*.

Alboquea Basque name for a *pibgorn* or *pibcorn*.

Alpenhorn, alphorn Long wooden horn with a mouthpiece giving the basic harmonics of its note. Some straight, some curved, varying lengths. 37

Althorn Another name for the *baritone*.

Alto High. See under *clarinet*, *fagotto* (*bassoon*), *flute*, *horn*, *oboe*, *saxophone*, *trombone*.

American organ Type of *harmonium* with various modifications to produce a more uniformly powerful sound.

Anvil (*Amboss*, Ger; *enclume*, Fr; *incudine*, Ital) A blacksmith's anvil (or metal bars on a resonant frame as a substitute) used for percussion effects.

Appollonicon A large organ that could be operated both manually and mechanically to imitate an orchestra, made in 1812.

Archlute A family of large double-necked *lutes*, including the *chitarrone* and *theorbo*.

Arpeggione A hybrid instrument, with 24 guitar-type frets and guitar tuning, it was a bass *viola da gamba* in essence and was bowed like a *cello*.

Aulos The Greek double-pipes of great antiquity, probably the same as the *halil* mentioned in the Bible. Consisted of two slender double-reed pipes played simultaneously, with three or four finger-holes, one pipe held in each hand.

Aura A patented type of *hand-harmonica* or *accordion*.

Baganna The Abyssinian *lyre*.

Bagpipe A multifarious family of instruments in which a bag of air, fed by a blowpipe, is used as a reservoir to blow a melody or chanter pipe and several drones. Many national and regional variants.

Balalaika A kind of *guitar* used in Russia, with frets, three gut strings and a triangular body.

Bandoneon A square-bodied button *accordion* used as solo instrument in Argentinian orchestras.

Bandora A bass *cittern*, also called *pandora*.

Bandoura A multi-stringed instrument of a curious bottle-like shape used in Russia.

Bandurria A Spanish member of the *cittern* family with six double strings tuned in fourths.

Banjo Fretted stringed instrument developed in America, with a round belly made of vellum stretched over a wooden hoop.

Various kinds of solo and accompanying instruments.   137

Banjoline Simplified form of the *banjo* with single strings.   138

Banjulele Simplified *banjo* with *ukulele* tuning.   138

Baritone (*tenor*, Am; *baryton*, Fr) Brass instrument of the *euphonium* family, vertical bell, mid-range.   41

Baryton Stringed instrument similar to the *viola da gamba* with six bowed strings and forty sympathetic strings, some of which could be plucked. Haydn wrote about 180 pieces for the instrument.

Bass (*contrebasse*, Fr) Low-pitched instrument of the *euphonium* family. Also known as the *bombardon*. Usually an E♭ instrument, with an even deeper version in B♭.   41

Bassanelli Sixteenth-century double-reed instrument, a single tube with fingerholes.

Basset horn A tenor instrument of the *clarinet* family with a curved or jointed body and flared bell.   31

Bassoon (*basson*, Fr; *fagott*, Ger; *fagotto*, Ital) Bass instrument of the double-reed *oboe* family with U-shaped body and conical bore. 32

Biwa A Japanese *lute*, dating back to the second century BC.

Bombardon Another name for the bass member of the *euphonium* family.   41

Bongoes Small twin tunable drums of the *conga* variety, held between the knees and played with the fingers.

Bow lute (*Pluriarc*, Fr) Early primitive *lute* with some *harp* characteristics, each string having a separate neck. The word bow refers to the general shape.

Bugle Simplest form of brass instrument, without keys, sounding the natural harmonics, usually with the tube coiled into something approximating trumpet shape.   37

Cabaca A gourd rattle with two gourds connected by a tube and encased in a network of beads. Also called *cabasa* and *chequeré*.

Carillon A set of bells played from a keyboard.

Castanets Small hollowed wooden clappers held in the palm and fingers, used as an accompaniment to Spanish dancing.   142

Celesta, celeste Small, soft-toned keyboard instrument, the sound produced by the hammers striking metal bars.

Cembalo German name for the *harpsichord*, Italian for the *zither*.

Chalumeau Small instrument of the *clarinet* family, developed at the same time, covering the high range of notes. 31

Charrasca Early percussion instrument, a scraper made from a bull's horn. Also known as *guiro*.

Chitarra battente Italian-style *guitar* with rounded back, wire-strung and played with a plectrum. 137

Chitarrone Large, bass instrument of the *lute* family, also known as the *Roman theorbo*. 135

Chyn Chinese *zither*.

Cimbalom Hungarian instrument of the *harp* family, the strings running across an open box, usually on legs, and hit with a pair of light and flexible beaters. 18, 138

Cithara Early Greek instrument of the *lyre* family. 13, 26

Cittern (*citole*, Early Eng; *cistré*, Fr; *cetera*, Ital; *Sister* or *Zitter*, Ger) A fretted string instrument, an early form of *guitar* with a shallow body and flat back. 135

Clarinet (*clarinette*, Fr; *Klarinette*, Ger; *clarinetto*, Ital) Single reed woodwind instrument invented at the beginning of the eighteenth century by J. C. Denner (1655–1707). 31

Clarinette d'amour A *clarinet* with a globular bell, now out of use.

Claves Cuban percussion instrument, a pair of wooden blocks held in the cupped hands and struck together. Equivalent of Spanish *castanet*.

Clavichord Keyboard instrument; forerunner of the *piano* with a brass blade or tangent striking the strings, and a soft tone. 45

Clavicor Brass instrument of the *euphonium* type patented in 1837.

Cobza Rumanian four-string *lute*.

Concertina Hand bellow instrument with buttons operating free reeds. 35

Cor anglais (*corno inglese*, Ital) A tenor *oboe* with a distinctive globular bell and double reed. 32

Cornet Instrument similar to the trumpet but with a larger bore and producing a mellower tone. 40

Cornett (*Zink*, Ger; *cornetto*, Ital; *cornet à bouquin*, Fr) An obsolete instrument, of the brass family, with similar kind of mouthpiece but generally made of wood and with fingerholes on the horn like a woodwind instrument.   28, 29

Cornophone Brass instrument similar to the *saxhorn* with backward curving bell, patented in 1890.

Cornu Early Roman instrument, a simple hoop-like *horn*.

Courtaut Early double-reed instrument with a single pillar and fingerholes.   28

Crotales, crotala Small, finger-operated cymbals, dating back to Egyptian times.   142

Crowd (*crwth*, Welsh) Early English bowed *lyre*.

Crumhorn A consort of reed instruments; forerunner of the *oboe* with a large double reed which was covered by a cap and not actually touched by the lips.   28

Curtal English name for the *fagotto*, the forerunner of the *bassoon*.

Cymbals Instruments of antique origin; metal, soup-plate shaped discs, either clashed together or hit singly.   142

Darabuka Cup-shaped drum of the *kettledrum* type found in North Africa and Egypt.

Davul Bass drum used in Turkey and the Balkan states.

Didjeridoo Primitive *trumpet* used by the Australian aborigines.

Domra Russian instrument of the *cittern* family.   137

Double-bass (*contrabasso*, Ital; *Kontrabass*, Ger; *contrebasse*, Fr) The largest member of the *violin* family, still retaining some viol characteristics.   20, 25

Doucaine Early double-reed instrument, now obsolete. Also called *dulzaina*.

Drum Percussion instrument with parchment head or heads stretched over a circular body.   141

Dulce melos, echiquier d'Angleterre Early keyboard instrument with the strings struck by a wooden jack.

Dulcimer Instrument with horizontal sounding board and strings played with hammers. Numerous variants.   18, 138

Dulzian Another name for the *fagotto*.

Endongo An African *lyre* from Ganda and Soga.

English guitar Another name for the *cittern* used in the seventeenth century.

Estives An early *bagpipe*.

Euphonium Brass instrument with upward pointing bell, a tenor *tuba*. 41

Fagotto The early form of the *bassoon*. 28

Fiddle A name generally applied to instruments of the bowed string category and to the smaller *violins* used for dancing. 21, 26

Fidla A three-stringed bowed *lyre* or *zither* from Iceland.

Fife Simple pipe used in folk music and in quasi-military bands. 29

Flageolet French name for a particular kind of recorder. There was also a British *flageolet* with different fingering. Had a vogue during the quadrille boom and was often referred to as the '*quadrille flageolet*'.

Flugelhorn (*ficorno*, Ital) Similar to the *trumpet* or *cornet* but larger and with a bigger bore. Used in German bands.

Flute (*flauto*, Ital; *Flöte*, Ger; *flûte*, Fr) A family of instruments consisting of a straight tube with fingerholes with or without keys, side blown over an aperture at one end. The 'end-blown' *flute* is another term for instruments of the *recorder* type. 29

Fortepiano Name, mainly used in England, for the early *pianoforte* prior to 1800. 47

Frame drum General name for *drums* of the flat-sided variety as distinct from the *kettledrums*.

Gadulka A Bulgarian *rebec*.

Gambang kayu Indonesian *marimba*.

Gender Metal-keyed *xylophone*.

Gittern Medieval form of *guitar*. 136

Glass harmonica A series of tuned glass bowls on a treadle with the sound produced by the dampened fingers.

Glockenspiel A xylophone-type instrument with steel bars struck with hammers. The *lyra glockenspiel* is an upright version in a *lyre*-like frame used in marching bands. 139

Gong A rimmed metal plate struck with a hammer. 143

Gora A Hottentot instrument in which a string is set in vibration by the lips vibrating an attached quill.

Ground instruments *Bows*, *zithers*, etc., using a hole in the ground as their sound box, mainly in African music.

Guimbarde Another name for the *Jew's harp*.

Guiro A serrated gourd which is scraped with percussive effect.

Guitar (*chitarra*, Ital; *Guitarre*, Ger; *guitare*, Fr; *Guitarra*, Portuguese) Fretted stringed instrument, mainly developed in Spain, with the strings plucked. A development of the *lute*.   135, 136

Guitarillo A five-string smaller version of the *guitar*.   137

Gusli A medieval *psaltery* still used in Russia.

Harding, harding fiddle A small *violin*-shaped instrument with sympathetic strings used in Norway.

Harmonica A name generally used for portable free-reed instruments, the most popular form being the *mouth-organ*. Also used in France and Germany to denote instruments of the *xylophone* type. See also *glass harmonica*.   35

Harmonium A small keyboard instrument of the *organ* family using reeds, the wind generally supplied by foot pedals.

Harp (*arpa*, Ital; *Harfe*, Ger; *harpe*, Fr) Multi-stringed instrument with a very long history and national variations.   12, 43

Harp-guitar, harp-lute, harp-zither Simplified forms of *harp* employing the principles of other instruments.   17

Harpsichord (*clavicembalo, gravicembalo, arpicordo*, Ital; *Cembalo, Clavicimbel, Kielflügel, Clavier, Flügel*, Ger; *clavecin*, the smaller models are also called *virginale* or *épinette*, Fr) Keyboard instrument in which the strings are plucked. Generally with two manuals and pedals and stops.   18, 44

Heckelphone A patented *cor anglais* with larger bore and different timbre, made in 1904.   33

Helicon General name for circular brass instruments.

Hibernicon Early English instrument of the *serpent* family.   37

Horn (*cor, cor d'harmonie*, Fr; *corno*, Ital; *Horn, Waldhorn*, Ger; *trompa*, Sp) Very general name for a variety of brass instruments. The modern orchestral horn is more generally referred to as the *French horn*.   40

Hornpipe A *reed pipe* utilising a cowhorn. Also in *bagpipe* form.

Hummel A Swedish *zither*.

Hurdy-gurdy (*simphonie chifonie*, Fr; *Leier*, Ger; *organistrum*, Ital) Fretted string instrument with the strings stopped by keys and the strings sounded by a rotating wheel.   145

Hwuchyn A Chinese *fiddle*.

Hydraulus Early Greek and Roman *organ* with the air forced through the pipes by water pressure.

Jew's harp Small lyre-shaped metal instrument held in the teeth with a strip of metal vibrated by a finger and the note formed by the shape of the mouth. Also known as a *guimbarde*.

Jingling Johnny A Turkish *tambourine*.

Kantele A Finnish *dulcimer*, played *zither* fashion.

Kaval Rim-blown *flute* from the Balkans.

Kazoo (*mirliton*, Fr) A small cigar-shaped instrument with a vibrating tissue, the note produced by the player's vocal cords.

Kettledrum Various kinds of basin-shaped drums with parchment tops capable of being tuned to basic notes. The name now refers to the military kind, the orchestral type being called *timpani*.   140

Key bugle A bugle with keys added. Forerunner of the *trumpet*, *cornet*, etc.   40

Koto National instrument of Japan. A large *zither* with thirteen strings plucked with a plectrum.

Langeleik Norwegian *zither*.

Laud A Spanish fretted instrument of the *cittern* family.   137

Lira da braccio A forerunner of the *violin*.   21

Lituus A Roman *horn*, rather like an *alphorn*.

Lur A bronze age *horn* similar to the above, tusk-shaped.

Lute (*lauto*, *leuto*, *liuto*, Ital; *Laute*, Ger; *luth*, Fr) Early fretted instrument, forerunner of the *guitar* and *mandolin*, with a rounded body resembling the latter.   15, 134

Lyra Greek *lyre* with a tortoiseshell body.   13

Lyre Ancient instrument, a forerunner of the *harp*. The strings are tuned in a fixed sequence of chords for accompaniment and strung between two arms. 12

Machada A simplified Portuguese *guitar*.

Mandolin, mandoline Italian instrument of the *lute* family with pear-shaped body and paired strings, plucked with a plectrum and often played with a tremolo effect. 13, 137

Mandora French and Italian name for a small kind of *lute*. 137

Maracas Rhythm instrument from Cuba and other South American countries; a pair of gourds filled with dried seeds and shaken.

Marimba A soft-toned S. American *xylophone*, with resonators. 139

Mellophone American name for a *tenor horn*. Also known as *tenor cor*.

Melodeon A simple type of free-reed *accordion*.

Melodica A chromatic *mouth-organ* with a keyboard.

Mélophone A *guitar*-shaped, bellows-operated instrument of the *concertina* family invented in France in 1834.

Metallophone A general name for instruments of the *xylophone* family with metal bars.

Monochord A single-string instrument with a movable bridge to produce varying single notes; an early teaching instrument. 45

Mouth-organ A portable, mouth blown, free-reed *harmonica*. 35

Musette A small French *bagpipe*. 34

Musical bow Primitive instrument like a hunting bow with the note obtained by varying the tension of the string.

Musical box Mechanical instrument with metal teeth operated by pins set in a rotating barrel. 146

Musical saw An ordinary carpenter's saw held between the knees and played on the smooth edge by a bow, the notes obtained by flexing the blade at varying tensions.

Nakers, naqqara Small Arabian *kettledrums*. 140

Nay An Arabian rim-blown *flute*.

Oboe (*hoboe*, Ital; *hautbois*, Fr) Wind instrument with conical bore, key fingering and double reed. The *oboe d'amore* is an instrument of lower pitch. The *oboe da caccia* was an early *cor anglais*.   32

Ocarina Small wind instrument made of wood, pottery or moulded material, blown through one corner and with fingerholes.   30

Ophicleide A bass *bugle*, used in orchestras from about 1819, eventually replaced by the *tuba*.   40

Organ Keyboard instrument, generally with two or more manuals operating flue and reed pipes, blown by hand or mechanically pumped bellows. Great variety from the simple portative organ to the modern electric.   129

Orpharion A variation of the *cittern*.   136

Pandoura Greek name for the *lute*.

Panpipe Set of reed pipes bound together and fingered with both hands.

Physharmonica Small reed *organ* made in Vienna in 1818.

Piano, pianoforte (*Hammerklavier*, Ger) Keyboard instrument with hammers striking the strings. Made in various forms, e.g. *grand, baby grand, upright, miniature*, and various eccentric versions. Earlier models sometimes known as *fortepiano*.   46

Piano accordion (*fisarmonica*, Ital) *Accordion* with piano-type keyboard.   35

Piccolo (*piccola, flauto piccolo, ottavino*, Ital; *Kleine Flöte, Oktaflöte*, Ger; *petite flûte*, Fr) A small, high-pitched *flute*.   30

Pipe Any kind of simple end blown, reed or reedless instrument. Popularly used (as in the *fife*) with a small drum called a *tabor* for dancing and marching purposes. A number of pipes are specifically called '*tabor pipes*'.   29

Plagiaulos Transverse *flute* from Sicily.

Pommer A medieval bass *shawm*.   33

Post horn Originally a long straight horn blowing the fundamental harmonics. Later in coiled form. With valves added it became the French *cornet de poste, cornet simple* or *cornet-à-pistons* and the English *cornopean* or *cornet*. Predecessor of the *French horn*.   39

Psaltery A cross between a *zither* and a *harp* with the strings across a flat sound-box and two bridges.   17, 139

Pyipar A Chinese *lute*.

Qanun A kind of *dulcimer*, generally Egyptian.   139
Quinton A short-lived hybrid *viol*-cum *violin*.

Rabab A primitive kind of *fiddle* with one or two strings, found in Arab countries.
Racket A double-reed instrument with a short, squat tubular body and numerous fingerholes.
Rebec A bowed *lute* from Greece and popular in Europe around the thirteenth century. Also *rubebe* from *rabab* (see above).   21, 27
Recorder (*flauto dolce, flauto diritto*, Ital; *Blockflöte, Schnabelflöte*, Ger; *flûte douce, flûte à bec*, Fr) A family of end-blown *flutes*, commonly found in soprano, descant, alto or treble, tenor and bass forms.   29
Reedpipe Originally a *pipe* cut from a reed, appearing in various forms in early musical cultures.
Requinte A small *guitar* used for accompaniment.   137
Rubebe Arabic name for the *rebec*.

Sackbut Instrument which became known, virtually unchanged, as the *trombone*.   37
Samisen Japanese long-necked *lute*.
Sansa Early instrument with plucked metal tongues.
Sarangi Indian bowed *lute* or *fiddle*.   150
Saron Indonesian metal-keyed *xylophone*.
Sarrusophone Metal double-reed instrument intended as an alternative to the *oboe* or *bassoon* in military bands; akin to the *saxophone*.
Saxhorn A family of brass instruments of the *cornet* and *euphonium* family with deeper cup mouthpieces and conical bores. Invented by Adolphe Sax 1842–5 as a standardised family mainly for military band use.   41
Saxophone A hybrid instrument with single-reed and woodwind keys but made of metal, introduced by Sax in 1846. The commonest forms are *soprano* (straight), *alto, tenor, baritone* and *bass*. Found most favour in popular music and jazz.   36

Scheitholt An early Alpine form of the *zither*.

Seraphine A form of reed *organ*, less popular than the *harmonium*.

Serpent A bass *cornett* of considerable length compressed into an undulating shape. Generally of wood covered with leather, it had a brass-type mouthpiece and woodwind-type keys. There were various types, such as the English *hibernicon, serpentcleide*; the French *serpent piffault, serpent forveille, ophibaryton, ophimonocleide*; and the German *Russian bassoon, chromatisches Basshorn, bass-euphonium.* 36

Shawm Ancestor of the *oboe* with fingerholes and a hard double reed producing a harsh, penetrating sound. Variants are still used in European folk music, e.g. the *tenora* in the Spanish *cobla* or sardana bands. 28, 29

Sheng Chinese *mouth-organ*.

Sho Japanese *mouth-organ*.

Sistrum South American *rattle*.

Sitar Popular instrument in India, a form of long-necked *lute* with seven metal strings and frets. 150

Sordoni (*Sordunen*, Ger; *courtauts*, Fr) Double-reed instrument of the *crumhorn* type. 28

Sousaphone A *tuba* adapted for marching, made to coil round the body and with a wide forward pointing bell.

Spinet A simplified form of the *harpsichord* with one string to each note. Made for domestic use. 44, 45

Swanee whistle Small *pipe* working on a *trombone* principle with sliding plunger to produce a glissando.

Syrinx Another name for the *panpipe*.

Tabor Small bowl-like *drum* generally used as accompaniment to *pipe* or *fife*. 141

Taile de hautbois An ancestor of the *cor anglais*, a tenor *oboe*.

Tamboritsa Persian long-necked *lute*.

Tambourine (*Tamburin, Bakische Trommel, Schellentrommel*, Ger; *tambourin*, Fr; *tamburino*, Ital) Small one-sided *drum* with small pairs of *cymbals* let into its sides, giving a rattling effect when hit or shaken. 142

Tambura Indian long-necked *lute*, similar to the sitar but without frets. 150

Tam-tam A large flat *gong* from the Far East. 143

Tarogato Hungarian instrument similar to a *soprano-saxophone* but made of wood and with fingerholes.

Tenore A small, higher-pitched *guitar* used in Spain. 137

Theorbo An elaborate form of *lute* with a second set of bass strings carried on an extra peg-box. Also called *theorbo lute*. 135

Tibia Short slender pipes used in pairs in Roman times.

Timbrel An early instrument similar to the *tambourine*; also known as *tof*.

Timpani (*timbales*, Fr; *Pauken*, Ger) Orchestral *kettledrums*, capable of flexible tuning. Recent models have a pedal which can produce a glissando and immediate tuning. 140

Triangle (*triangolo*, Ital; *Triangel*, Ger) A piece of metal bent into an unclosed triangle and struck with a metal rod. 142

Tromba marina A form of *monochord* used in European folk music.

Trombone (*Posaune*, *Zugposaune*, Ger) Brass instrument with a unique system of overlapping slides to lengthen the tubing and produce the required notes. Originally known as the *sackbut*. 37

Trumpet (*tromba*, *tromba ventile*, *clarino*, Ital; *Trompete*, Ger; *trompette*, *trompette à pistons*, Fr) An elaborated *bugle* with valves, the leading member of the brass family. 39

Tuba Brass instrument that looks like a very large *cornet* with the bell pointing upwards. Most used form is the *bass-tuba*. The *tenor-tuba* is more generally referred to as the *euphonium* or *Baryton* (Ger). A marching version is the *sousaphone*. 40, 41

Tympanum Ancient *drum* like a *tambourine* without jingles. 142

Ukulele, ukelele A small member of the *guitar* family originating in Hawaii. *Ukulele-banjo* is a *banjo* with *ukulele* tuning. 138

Vibraphone Similar to the *xylophone* but has a small fan electrically revolved in each resonator to produce a pronounced vibrato when required. 139

Viella (*Vièle*, Fr; *viola*, Ital) A five-string troubadour fiddle used around the thirteenth century.

Vihuela Ancestor of the Spanish guitar, a flat-backed kind of *viol*, in two versions – *vihuela de mano* (plucked) and *vihuela de arco* (bowed). 136

Vina Instrument from Northern India. A curious kind of *zither* with two large gourd resonators. 150

Viols A family of stringed instruments, flat-backed, usually with six strings and frets. The instrument rested on the knees and the bow was held underneath. A consort of *viols* was referred to as a '*chest*'. The *bass viol* or *viola da gamba* was the last to be used regularly, eventually supplanted by the cello. Not really ancestors of the *violin* family but developed concurrently. 21

Viola (*Bratsche*, Ger; *alto*, Fr) An alto *violin*, a larger instrument of the same construction tuned a fifth lower. 24

Viola da gamba Member of the *viol* family. 22

Viola d'amore A cross between a *violin* and a *viol* with extra vibrating strings. 22

Violin (*violino*, Ital; *Violine*, *Geige*, Ger; *violon*, Fr) The leading member of the violin string family, unfretted keyboard and played with a horsehair bow. Occasionally referred to as the *fiddle* (*Fiedel*, Ger). 20, 22

Violoncello, 'Cello (*Violoncell*, Ger; *violoncelle*, Fr) A bass *violin*, twice the length of the ordinary *violin* and played with its tailpiece resting on the floor. Uses a heavier bow. 24

Violone An early name for *bass viol* and later applied to the *double-bass*.

Virginals (*virginale*, *épinette*, Fr) An earlier and smaller version of the *harpsichord* built in an oblong case with the strings running from left to right. Some were small enough to be held on the lap. The strings are plucked as in the *harpsichord* action. 44, 45

Wagner tuba Not really a *tuba* at all but more akin to the *horn*, invented by the composer for special effects. 41

Xylophone (*zilafone, gigelira*, Ital; *Strohfiedel, Holzharmonika*, Ger; *echelette, claquebois*, Fr) Tuned pieces of wood laid on a frame and struck by hammers. 139

Zampogna Italian *bagpipes.*

Zither Stringed instrument developing from the *harp* and *dulcimer*, the strings stretched across a resonant soundbox and plucked. A modified form with chords operated by pressing buttons is known as the *auto-harp* or *zither harp.* 138

Zurla A Macedonian *shawm.* 29

LIST OF COLOUR PLATES

165

Bibliography and Discography

of some of the principal instruments
(titles of books in italic, records in roman)

GENERAL

Baines, A. (ed.), *Musical Instruments Through the Ages* (Penguin, 1961).
Marcuse, S., *Musical Instruments: a Comprehensive Dictionary* (Country Life, 1966).

BASSOON

Camden, A., *Bassoon Technique* (OUP, 1962).
Langwill, L. G., *The Bassoon and Contrabassoon* (Benn, 1965).

CELLO

'The Cello' (Julian Lloyd-Webber, Clifford Benson), Discourses 'All About Music', ABK17.
'Encore' (Paul Tortelier, S. Iwasaki), HMV HQS1289.

CLARINET

Gilbert, R., *The Clarinettist's Solo Repertoire*, New York, 1972.
Rendall, F. G., *The Clarinet* (Benn, 1954).
Thurston, F., *Clarinet Technique* (OUP, 1956).
Williamson, R., *The Clarinet and Clarinet Playing*, New York, 1949.
'The Clarinet' (Jack Brymer), Discourses 'All About Music', ABK16.

CLAVICHORD

Russell, R., *The Harpsichord and Clavichord* (Faber, 1959).

FLUTE

Boisted and Chambers, *Essential Repertoire for Flute*, London, 1964.
Chapman, F. B., *Flute Technique* (OUP, 1958).

FRENCH HORN

Coar, B., *The French Horn*, Illinois, 1950.
Gregory, R., *The Horn* (Faber, 1961).
Morley Pegge, R., *The French Horn* (Benn, 1960).

GUITAR

Grunfeld, F. V., *The Art and Times of the Guitar*, New York and London, 1969.
Sharpe, A. P., *The Story of the Spanish Guitar* (Clifford Essex Music Co., 1968).
'The Classical Guitar' (John Mills), Discourses 'All About Music', ABK10.
'The World of the Spanish Guitar' (Narcisso Yepes), Decca SPA233; Vol. 2, SPA278.

HARP

Armstrong, R. B., *The Irish and Highland Harps*, New York, 1969.
Rensch, R., *The Harp, its History, Technique and Repertoire* (Duckworth, 1969).
'The Harp' (John Marson), Discourses 'All About Music', ABK15.

HARPSICHORD, SPINET, VIRGINALS

Boalch, D. H., *Makers of the Harpsichord and Clavichord, 1440–1840* (Reeves, 1956).
Russell, R., *The Harpsichord and Clavichord* (Faber, 1959).
'Historical Keyboard Instruments' (Spinets, Harpsichords and Pianos), Oryx, 1600 and 1811.

OBOE

Bate, P. A., *The Oboe* (Benn, 1956).
Rothwell, E., *Oboe Technique* (OUP, 1953).

ORGAN

Sumner, W. L. S., *The Organ, its Evolution, Principles of Construction and Use* (Macdonald, 1952).

Whitworth, R., *The Electric Organ*, London, 1948.

PERCUSSION

Blades, J., *Orchestral Percussion Technique* (OUP, 1974).

Blades, J., *Percussion Instruments and Their History* (Faber, 1973).

Kirby, P. R., *The Kettle-Drums* (OUP, 1930).

'Blades on Percussion', Discourses 'All About Music', ABK13.

PIANO

Harding, E. M., *The Pianoforte* (Cambridge University Press, 1933)

Matthews, D., *Keyboard Music*, London, 1973.

'The Piano' (Peter Katin), Discourses 'All About Music', ABK11.

SAXOPHONE

'The Krein Saxophone Quartet', Canon (S)CNN4983.

VIOLIN

Bachman, A., *An Encyclopaedia of the Violin*, London, 1929.

Van der Stracten, E., *The History of the Violin* (Cassell, 1933).

'The Glory of Cremona' (Ricci), Brunswick AXA4521, (S) SXA4521; or MCA. (Deleted.)

WOODWIND, BRASS

Baines, A., *Woodwind Instruments and Their History* (Faber, 1957).

Carse, A., *Musical Wind Instruments* (Macmillan, 1939).

INDIAN INSTRUMENTS

'Music from India', HMV ASD2295.

'Indian Music', TL5424/5.

'Indian Dance Music', Eros 8032.

ANCIENT MUSIC

'Music from the Time of Christopher Columbus', Philips SAL 3697.

'Music from the Time of the Crusaders', CBS 73083.

Collections of
musical instruments

GREAT BRITAIN

Barnard Castle Bowes Museum, Barnard Castle, Co. Durham. Early.

Belfast Ulster Museum, Stranmillis, Belfast BT9 5AB. General.

Birmingham Birmingham School of Music, Dale End, Birmingham B4 7LT. General. Part of L.L. Key Collection.
City Museum and Art Gallery, Dept. of Science and Industry, Newhall St., Birmingham 3. Mechanical instruments. Liddell collection of musical boxes.

Bradford Bolling Hall, Bolling Hall Rd., Bradford 4. Stringed and wind.

Bristol Mickleburgh Music Museum, Stokes Croft, Bristol 1. Mechanical instruments.

Broadway Snowshill Manor, nr. Broadway, Glouc. Wind, strings, early.

Cambridge Fitzwilliam Museum, Trumpington St., Cambridge. Stringed, keyboard and wind.
University Museum of Archaeology and Ethnology, Cambridge. Early instruments.

Canterbury Royal Museum, Beaney Institute, High St., Canterbury. Early.

Cardiff National Museum of Wales: Welsh Folk Museum, St. Fagans, nr. Cardiff. Stringed, keyboard and wind.

Carlisle Museum and Art Gallery, Tullie House, Castle St., Carlisle. Stringed and wind.

Chester Grosvenor Museum, Grosvenor St., Chester. Recorders.

Douglas Manx Museum, Library and Art Gallery, Douglas, IOM. Stringed, keyboard and wind.

Dundee City Art Gallery and Museum, Albert Institute, Albert Sq., Dundee. Simpson Collection of instruments.

Edinburgh National Museum of Antiquities of Scotland, 1 Queen St., Edinburgh 2. Stringed, keyboard and wind.

Reid School of Music, Alison House, Nicolson Sq., Edinburgh 8. Stringed, keyboard and wind. Reid Collection of flutes.

Royal Scottish Museum, Chambers St., Edinburgh 1. Stringed, keyboard and wind.

Scottish United Services Museum, The Castle, Edinburgh 1. Wind and percussion.

Glasgow Kelvingrove Museum and Art Gallery, Argyll St., Glasgow G3 8AG. General.

Hailsham Michelham Priory, Upper Dicker, Hailsham, Sussex. Mummery Collection of musical instruments, etc.

Halifax Bankfield Museum, Haley Hill, Halifax. General.

Huddersfield Tolson Memorial Museum, Ravensknowle Park, Wakefield Rd., Huddersfield. Wind.

Ipswich Christchurch Mansion, Christchurch Park, Ipswich. Stringed, keyboard and wind.

Keighley Cliffe Castle Art Gallery and Museum, Keighley. General.

Liskard Paul Corin, St. Keynes Mill, St. Keynes Station, nr. Liskard, Cornwall. Mechanical organs and other instruments.

London British Piano Museum, 368 High Street, Brentford, Middx. Keyboard, player pianos, mechanical, etc.

Fenton House, Hampstead Grove, London NW3. Early keyboard, etc.

Horniman Museum and Library, London Rd., Forest Hill, London SE23. General. Adam Carse and Percy A. Bull Collections.

London Museum, Kensington Palace, London W8. Stringed, keyboard and wind.

Royal College of Music, Prince Consort Rd., London SW7. General. Donaldson Collection.

Tower of London, London EC3. Wind and percussion.
Victoria & Albert Museum, South Kensington, London SW7. General.

Maidstone Museum and Art Gallery, Maidstone, Kent. Stringed, keyboard and wind.

Manchester Henry Watson Music Library, St. Peter's Sq., Manchester 2. Stringed, keyboard and wind. Henry Watson Collection.
Royal Manchester College of Music, Devas St., Manchester M15. Stringed, keyboard and wind.

Merthyr Tydfil Cyfarthfa Castle Art Gallery and Museum, Merthyr Tydfil, Glamorgan. General.

Norwich St. Peter Hungate Museum, Princes St., Norwich NOR 12J. Stringed, keyboard and wind (church).
Strangers' Hall Museum, Charing Cross, Norwich NOR 20J. Stringed, keyboard and wind.

Oxford Ashmolean Museum, Beaumont St., Oxford. General.
Pitt Rivers Museum, University Dept. of Ethnology and Prehistory, Parks Rd., Oxford. General, early.

St. Albans St. Albans Organ Museum, 326 Camp Road, St. Albans. Mechanical organs, etc.

Wigan Public Library, Rodney St., Wigan, Lancs. Rimmer Wind Collection.

York Castle Museum, York. Folk instruments, general.

AUSTRALIA

Sydney Museum of Applied Arts and Sciences, 659-695 Harris St., Broadway, 2007.

AUSTRIA

Salzburg Salzburg Museum, Museumplatz 1, Postfach 525, A-5010. Concerts, demonstrations and research on historical instruments.

GERMANY

Nuremberg Germanic National Museum, Kornmarkt 1.

ITALY

Genoa White Palace Gallery, Via Garibaldi 11, Paganini's violin.

NETHERLANDS

The Hague Municipal Museum of The Hague, Stadhouderslaan 41, 2076. Unique survey of instruments from four centuries and five continents. 2,600 instruments including Italian and Flemish harpsichords, and a complete gamelan orchestra from Indonesia.

NORWAY

Oslo Norwegian Folk Museum, Bygdöy, 2. Modern and primitive.

U.S.A.

MASSACHUSETTS

Boston Museum of Fine Arts, 465 Huntington Ave., 02115.

NEW YORK

New York The Metropolitan Museum of Art, Fifth Ave. at 82nd St., 10028.

OHIO

Cincinnati Cincinnati Art Museum, Eden Park, 45202.

PENNSYLVANIA

Philadelphia Museum of the Philadelphia Civic Center, 34th St. & Civic Center Blvd., 19104. Oriental and African.

TENNESSEE

Vermillion W.H. Over Dakota Museum, University of South Dakota, 57069. Arne B. Larson collection.

WISCONSIN

Green Bay Neville Public Museum, 129 South Jefferson St., 54301.

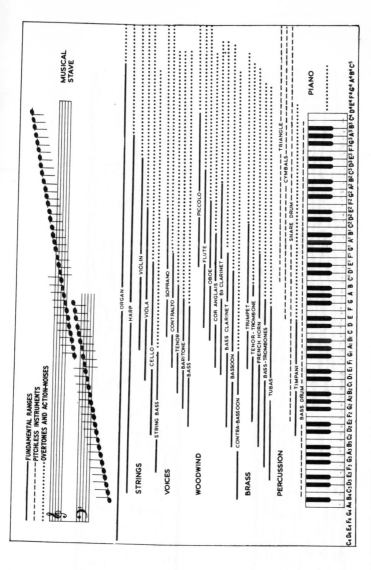

FREQUENCY COMPASS OF ORCHESTRAL INSTRUMENTS AND VOICES SHOWN IN RELATION TO THE MUSICAL STAVE.